TAKE IT

TO

THE

BRIDGE

ALBUMS BY J'MICHAEL PEEPLES

Enigma

Take It to the Bridge

TAKE IT
TO THE BRIDGE

J'Michael Peeples

JMP MOVEMENT

COLUMBIA, SOUTH CAROLINA

for

Clifford

Margrette

Hope

You are the soul behind these words

Praise the bridge that carried you over.

–George Colman

CONTENTS

MY FAMILY IS WHY I SING; WHEREVER I SING, I SING FOR THEM

The conductor demanded I play a complex concerto too cumbersome for my untrained hands. Only a master musician would have the resilience to make it to the coda without giving up.

"What are you worried about?" he asked.

"The concert is tomorrow." Knowing the room would be filled with devoted connoisseurs added to my anguish, too deep to articulate. "Is there a simpler composition I could play?" I asked.

By the look on his face, he wasn't sympathetic. Agitation and then what seemed like sadness filled the space between us. Leaving the composition on the music stand, the conductor turned to me and said, "I have guests waiting for you to guide them through the dissonant harmonies and unorthodox interludes that novice musicians fear. Don't give up before playing the first note."

"I DON'T FEEL NO WAYS TIRED"

I hadn't cried in a long time. I prided myself in being able to conceal pain, and for two hours, I stared in the bathroom mirror trying to convince myself that everything was going to be okay, but I was only fooling myself. I was so fidgety I cut myself shaving. Blood dripped from my cheek to the sink. In thirty minutes a hearse would be at our front door waiting to escort us to the funeral. I knew my wife and daughter would be looking to me for strength. I was so fragile that if my daughter hugged me I knew for certain I would break.

The doorbell rang. The time had come. My wife and daughter grabbed my hands and we walked out together. During the ride to the church we reminisced the moments we shared with Junior that brought us joy. Laughter soothed the agony but only for a moment. As we pulled up to the church, my daughter leaned over and said, "Together we're going to survive this."

With each step towards the church the burden of reality weighed heavy on me. I knew I would see hundreds of people with sorrow on their faces, so I kept my head lowered as I walked down the aisle. Even so the sound of mourning made it hard to breath. We sat on the front row, about ten feet from Junior's casket. I sat between my wife and daughter and wrapped my arms around them.

The time had come for me to look at my son one last time. My wife, daughter, and I held hands as we walked to the casket we'd chosen for him days ago. I had thought then that as a parent I had expected to choose what crib or bed my child would rest, not what casket. Here Junior was, nestled in his place of eternal rest. He was dressed in what he'd worn to prom earlier that spring. My wife had made her son an epic dark leather suit. He looked handsome, elegant even.

My daughter tucked between Junior's long fingers a picture of when she and her brother were kids playing baseball. Junior's first love had been baseball. He also loved music. As he grew, his list of passions grew to include muscle cars and a motorcycle I'd bought him earlier that spring and a girlfriend. Brooke was the only girl he'd brought home for us to meet, and she'd been his prom date. As I leaned to kiss my baby boy one last time, I noticed another photo, one from prom, tucked in the crook of his arm. It was a candid shot of Junior, kneeling as if he was on stage, had given the performance of a lifetime, and was taking a final bow before Brooke.

Walking away from the casket, I knew I would never be the same again. *God, take me and let my son live*, I had prayed over and over for the three days my son was on life support. Even when the doctor pronounced my son dead, I had still felt I could bargain with Death. Somehow the doctor was wrong and God would miraculously bring my son back to life.

I didn't pay attention to the eulogy. I was too distracted with memories of the two of us playing catch and fishing, of working on cars together, of the day I'd brought home a motorcycle for him. I recalled us getting dressed for church. Junior never liked going to children's church, he preferred sitting next to me for Sunday services. Typically, we sat on the front pew. It's the pew I now sat with what remained of our family. From this pew I watched him being christened and a few years later baptized. From this pew I saw him recite his first Easter speech and lead his first solo. It's from this pew that I imagined I'd watch him say, "I do" to his sweetheart.

I was paralyzed as I watched the ushers shut the casket, and if it wasn't for the choir singing, I would have remained seated until the last person left. With tears streaming down my face, I stood up, but I couldn't sing. When the congregation joined the choir for the final stanza, for a moment, I felt the weight of sorrow lift until we made our way outside to the graveyard. With the sound of dirt hitting the casket, the reality of never hearing my son's voice became real. My family would have to figure out how to live without Junior, but without him, there'd be no song.

INTRO

I was on, again, my third day without sleep. My wife was sound asleep when I decided to leave the house. Small voices charmingly whispered what sounded like a better alternative than coping with what had become a daily internal turbulence. I'd never had a drink in my life, but I drove to the nearest convenience store to purchase what I thought would be enough alcohol to sedate my thoughts.

I drove to a bridge not far from where I lived that separated the city folks from the country folks. Underneath the bridge is where cast-downs and vagrants gathered to drink, hoping, I assumed, to escape their reality. In the past, as I crossed this particular bridge, I'd look out of my window with haughty eyes. These men were weak. They couldn't keep it together, could they? It had been easy to cast judgment, and, oh, how I'd judged these men.

Now, for me, there was a different sort of judgment. Under my driver's seat was my .38 special, fully loaded. With spirits in one hand and my .38 in the other, I made my way down to the bottom of the bridge without any concern of whether I would see the sun again. I didn't want another sunrise. I didn't fear the darkness or the men-like zombies who staggered past me. I sat down and drank bottle after bottle. As if it were a mantra, I repeated over and over: *I don't want to be here, I don't want to be here. Take me, take me, take me. Please leave my boy, please leave my boy. Take me...*

When I tried to stand, I fell back to the ground in a stupor. I twirled my .38 around and around on my middle finger. I was so drunk that I had to close my eyes to keep everything from spinning in circles. I pressed my head to the ground, as if I might permanently stake a claim to the bridge above. Then I drifted.

Proud parents stood at a fence cheering on a team.

Even though baseball is unarguably a team sport, within each parent's heart is a selfish hope that his or her child will hit the game-winning homerun.

I watch closely, as a young boy takes warm-up swings in the batter's box. He keeps his eyes on the pitcher while squaring his shoulders, rocking back and forth, adjusting to the pitcher's rhythm.

"Batter up!" the umpire yells.

The score is 3 to 5, bases loaded with two outs in the last inning. The boy turns to me for approval.

"Keep your eyes on the ball, son."

Unlike the other parents, I remain cool and I remain

seated in the bleachers. Junior has taken interest in the game at an early age. He's carried my glove and bat for me ever since he could walk. I've trained him well, which gives him an advantage over the other kids.

I am a little nervous for him only because he is the last one up to bat, but I'm confident in his ability to "put the bat on the ball," as the old timers put it

"Strike one!" the umpire screamed as the opposing team rejoices.

Junior swings at the ball, as if he is trying to hit a mosquito. The fastball sounds like a gunshot when it hits the catcher's mitt. I signal for Junior to calm down. He doesn't need to knock the ball out of the park. He needs to relax and make contact.

"Strike two!" the empire screams.

Strike two clocked in at 70mph.

Junior takes a step back from the plate to reposition his posture. He doesn't appear worried at all and maintains his poise even though the odds are against him. He turns to gaze at the crowd. I can see his eyes searching for reassurance in my eyes. I nod as if I am giving him permission. He slowly walks back to the plate. He points his bat at the pitcher then raises his bat towards the sky. The ballpark gets real quiet and by the look on the pitcher's face I only hope he doesn't try to hit Junior with the ball.

Pointing the bat at a pitcher is the ultimate insult. Parents and the coaches look at me as if I have something to do with Junior's boldness. I am just as surprised as they were. Junior looks at me one more time and smiles. By the way he digs his cleats into the clay and positions the torque in his shoulders, I know something special is about to happen.

The parent to my right leans over and whispers, "Is that your son? Does he normally do that and how often has it worked?" she asks.

"How much money do you have on this game?" I ask kindly.

She's startled by my question. She clears her throat and sits up straight. "I don't place bets."

"Well, ma'am, you should." I stand up and start clapping and then look at the parent to my right and smile. She returns the smile and stands to clap along with me. Then other parents join in.

As the pitcher winds up, I can see a seriousness in his

eyes and feel the heat that is about to be released from his arm. He looks left, right, and raises his leg high. The crowd hears the pitcher's grunt as he cocks his arm back to throw. What's even louder is the sound of the bat meeting the ball. Junior has so much confidence in his swing he doesn't move from home plate. The ball is lost in the lights but I know it has cleared the fence.

"Wish you'd placed that bet," I said to the woman to the right of me.

She laughs. All the parents on our team stand and cheer for him as he rounds third base and heads home. No sooner does he touch home plate, he runs over to me and wants to celebrate. As much as I want to jump for joy with him, I encourage him to go celebrate with his team first.

When I woke, I immediately sobered up. My .38 lying peacefully on my chest with the barrel pointing at my face. I took a deep breath, grabbed the .38, emptied the rounds, and threw my handgun in the lake. During the drive home all I could think about was the dream. It had been pretty accurate, but there was something I didn't understand.

I like to tell myself you are the wind
It eases my mind, each gust that Graces my skin is your kiss,
It brings me a smile

> *Picked up the phone*
> *Expecting bad news again*
> *Let me off this roller coaster*
> *When will this ride end?*

The sun crept into my bathroom and sliced through the darkness. I didn't need the bathroom light to shave. I assumed it would be hot outside, but to my surprise the temperature was perfect. A cool breeze made the summer day feel like the cusp of spring. We Southerners only pray for days like this. God often ignores our petitions. I learned to get along with the heat, even though it was always on my back. When I was younger and complained about the heat, my grandmother would say, "It's God's way of showing you a glimpse of Hell, so you betta act right, boy."

To my surprise, my wife had taken my favorite suit and dress shirt to the cleaners. After showering I noticed both lay across the bed, still covered with plastic. This wasn't just any suit. My wife had tailored it to fit my tall, slender frame. I felt confident and smooth. So smooth that I did a double take to see if the mirror would give me a compliment.

My wife kissed me goodbye. She grabbed me, pulled me in close, and laid a big, fat kiss on me. The kind of kiss distant lovers give one another after months apart. I was sad I couldn't take her with me. Hugging me tight while standing at the door, she wished me luck. She thought I had an interview for a promotion. I'd misled her with the best intentions.

Some might call it chance, but I'd like to think God manipulated circumstances so I got off to a good start. The drive took about thirty minutes. I was in no rush to get to the appointment so I took the scenic route through town and stayed in the slow lane once I got on the highway. With one hand on the steering wheel and the other hanging out the window, I whistled along to Al Green's "Let's Stay Together." It was one of my and my wife's favorite songs. I kept rewinding the tape until I reached the counselor's office. I wanted to maintain a strong façade so I could get a clean bill of health.

I arrived a few minutes early but instead of waiting in the lobby until my appointment, I stayed in the car. There I rehearsed my answers, assuming the doctor would ask me to describe my symptoms. Smile before answering, I told myself while practicing in the rearview mirror. I had never been to a counselor before. My father counseled us before we got married, but those had been brighter times. I figured if God and I couldn't come to a resolution over my personal problems, surely no counselor could help me. My biggest fear was being misdiagnosed and growing dependent on antidepressants when all I needed was sympathy, empathy, or a pat on the back.

I imagined walking into the counselor's office to find a tall white gentleman with hair combed to the side to cover a bald spot. He'd most likely wear square-framed reading glasses. Being watched by two sets of eyes, I assumed would feel weird. *Just stare at the crown of his head*, I repeatedly told myself. Then there's the yellow memo pad. We all know it's mostly a sketchpad. A nod here and there, only pretending to listen while the client pours his heart out. Not a bad job, getting paid to listen. I said a prayer, *Dear God, if this man can't help me, send me someone who can.*

As I walked to the door, I thought about how weird it was to ask God to use another human to help me. That alone nearly made me turn around and head back to my car. But I was here, and there was no turning back.

After knocking on the door I noticed an older gentleman waiting as if he was either a greeter or waiting to valet my car. Dark skin, interesting grey eyes, and curly hair, he fit the description of being a mix of Native and African American. His face was adorned with deep wrinkles that suited him like a vintage leather jacket seems to suit rebels and heroes alike. He had a muscular frame that complimented his height. By his stature you would assume he might have played tight end.

I reached in my coat pocket to grab the counselor's card to make sure I was at the right location. With my eyebrows raised and cheeks clinched, I asked, "Excuse me, sir, is this 8513 Westchester Street?"

He smiled and pointed at the street sign and then pointed to the engraved address on the front door. "I can read, sir," I replied. "Your head was blocking the sign on the door."

The old man reached for me with both arms extended, as if he was welcoming his lost son home. It struck me that this might be some deranged mental patient. But I truly didn't care. If he attacked me, I knew it would bring me some amount of relief to sock him.

"Clifford, come on in!" I froze because he'd said my name as if he'd been awaiting my arrival since last week.

"Yes, sir," I replied as he reached to shake my hand.

His hands felt like a worn-out baseball glove that had snagged a lot of balls from going over the fence. I was now face-to-face with him, so close that I could see the details of his skin and the wrinkles around his eyes. I couldn't deny his father-like smile and gentle spirit.

The old man escorted me into the waiting room.

"Clifford, would you like some coffee?" he asked.

"No thanks, but water would be nice."

While he was gone, I investigated the waiting room, scanning the magazines and paintings on the wall. Music played in the background. There was a really nice painting on the wall of three women being hugged by one man. Looked to be a wife and two daughters. Even though it was only a painting, the eyes of the man looked very familiar.

"Here you go," the old man said as he poured water from a pitcher into a mason jar. "Let me know if you would like a refill."

"No, sir, this'll be fine, but you might want to give the plant a little water. It look a little thirsty," I replied pointing to a sad looking fern.

"You're right. I tend to talk to ferns more than water them. I guess it comes with the territory." With that the old man let out a hearty laugh.

After ten minutes had passed, I grew impatient.

"Am I early for my appointment?" I asked.

"The doctor will be with you shortly," the old man replied. "How about a game of chess while you wait?"

Before I could answer, he pulled up a seat across from me and placed a chessboard on the coffee table between us. I wasn't in the mood to play, but chess was one of my favorites. The board was set, and all we had to do was agree on who would make the first move. I was taught to show my elders respect, but most of the old men I knew were tricksters who kept a spare ace, a pocketknife, and a two-headed coin on them at all times, so I suggested he make the first move.

He refused, then pulled a coin from his pocket, and said, "Let's let fate decide."

I agreed to let fate decide as long as he allowed me to flip the coin and let me pick heads. Heads it was. I was about to secure the first move, but before my fingers could touch a pawn, a tap on the shoulder broke my focus. I looked over my shoulder, and there he was standing with square frame reading glasses and a yellow memo pad tucked under his arm.

"All therapists do look alike," I whispered under my breath.

The old man looked at me and smiled, then he shook my hand, and said that he would leave the game as is until next time. Even though I had no plans of coming back, I returned a smile with a smile. I had almost made it to the other room before he got my attention.

"Catch this," he said. Inside my hand was the quarter that decided who made the first move. "My name is Nathaniel Jefferson. Keep the change," he said.

"Nice to meet you, Nathaniel. Um, thanks," I said this awkwardly, too nervous for my first session to respond any differently to this strange old guy and his strange ways.

"Nathaniel is great. He knows how to make new patients feel comfortable, don't you think?" suggested my counselor. I cleared my throat.

"I guess," I replied.

Frankly I was mildly annoyed the game had been interrupted, but then I hadn't come there to play games. I wanted this counseling session to be quick and straight to the point like a routine checkup with my physician. Diagnose the symptoms and prescribe the meds.

He escorted me to a comfy loveseat inside his office. It was hard to resist reclining once you sat down.

"Feel free to kick your feet up," he said.

I sat on the sofa as if it was a hard wooden chair, even twitched a little bit to make it clear to him that no amount of comfort would make me feel at ease.

"Clifford Alexander is your name correct?"

"Yes," I replied. "I was born September 12, 1940 at three o'clock in the morning in a small country hospital. My mother said I was so dark-skinned, that if it wasn't for my blue eyes, I would of blended right in with the black shirt my father was wearing. Instead of saying how cute I was as a newborn, she is said to have repeated over and again: 'Lewd, he is black.' To this day, my family calls me Black."

I continued to blabber information he hadn't ask for. He continued to take notes on his yellow memo pad, no matter how out of sequence the things I said were. I didn't mention my son or his death, I talked about other things, inconsequential things. Things I hadn't thought about in years. I talked about the music I liked and how I was a churchgoer and that my father was a pastor, but that after I had married my wife I'd decided she and I should attend a church other than my father's. I told him that my mother grew tomatoes and that whenever I was over visiting her she'd make me sing her favorite praise songs. The counselor seemed to make a shorthand note of every detail I offered. I couldn't help myself. I was curious.

"Are you really taking notes?" I asked.

He reassured me that he was. "With all of my patients, yes. I will review our sessions so I can have a deeper understanding. It helps me do my job well."

Hearing this I thought I'd relax, but I was still anxious and ended the session early. While I hadn't offered anything of consequence, I was, for some reason, glad I had come. I wasn't sure whether or not I'd return. Emotionally I was in neutral, but I was okay with being in neutral. It felt good to communicate with someone something that resembled honesty. I hadn't lied. Not once. Maybe I wasn't being forthright, I hadn't said, "Hey, Doc, my son died, and I don't want to go on living." Nor had I divulged that I had drunk myself into a stupor, and, in that stupor, had put serious thought to blowing my brains out or that, sober, every single time I came to a bridge, any bridge, I did the math to see if I would survive a jump. No, there's a difference between honesty and truth, and sharing that sort of truth took its own brand of honesty, and I wasn't ready, not yet.

In the lobby, as I was leaving, Nathaniel tried to get me to schedule my next appointment. I made an excuse about work keeping me busy and told him that I'd call him later in the week.

Hours had passed since my first counseling session. I couldn't explain or even remember where the day had gone. I'd taken a drive out to the country. I'd revved the engine to the red line, going miles and miles, before shifting gears to slow down some when I came upon the city limits of small towns. Now, heading home, I'd race the sunset. I didn't want to explain why I was late coming home on a Friday. I certainly wouldn't bother her with the detail that I hadn't made the slightest effort to make an appearance at the office in the first place, much less explain to them my absence.

I checked my rearview mirror and merged onto the interstate. Before I knew it, I was at eighty-five. I gripped tightly the steering wheel, as my car trembled. About a mile or so up the road, a highway patrolmen's car hid near an overpass. I took my foot off the gas hoping I wouldn't get clocked, but as I approached the vehicle, it became clear that what I thought was a police car only looked like a police car. It was actually a station wagon. Soon I came upon a man walking towards the direction I'd come. After I passed, a voice in my head directed me to, "Look in the rearview mirror."

I got off the next exit so I could circle back. I raced around the intersection then pulled over and parked a few hundred feet behind the car. I saw the man putting a jack under the car. I got out of the my car and walked towards him.

"Nathaniel, is that you?" I asked as I walked a little closer. "Can I give you a hand?"

Whoever the man was either hadn't heard me or wasn't paying attention, so I turned around to walk back to my car only to find there were blue lights and drawn weapons pointed at me.

"Put your hands up!" an officer yelled.

I obeyed their orders and placed both hands behind my head.

"Do you have any weapons?" the same officer asked.

"No, sir," I replied.

A female officer walked towards me, while the other officer took down my license plate.

"What did I do?" I asked.

It was obvious she was frustrated. Her hair was pulled back tightly. By the looks of her waistline, she was probably a regular at the donut shop. I kept all my thoughts to myself while she frisked me. Since she'd gotten out the passenger side, I knew who was really in charge. It was a good five minutes before the other officer walked towards us. Surprisingly, he had a smile. He walked right past us. When I turned to see what was going on, I saw the officer hugging Nathaniel, as if they hadn't seen each other in years. They laughed loudly. Their bond seemed brotherly. They couldn't be kin, I thought, as I tried to interpret their relationship.

"Did I break a law?" I asked the female officer.

"What do you want me to do with this guy?" she asked the other officer who was so caught up chatting with Nathaniel that he ignored his walkie-talkie's page. When they made their way over to us, the officer ignored me and introduced Nathaniel to his partner.

I remained quiet, until the officer reached in his back pocket, grabbed his ticket book, and started writing me a ticket.

"What's the — ?" I asked.

Nathaniel interrupted and mentioned I was a good friend. The officer gave me a verbal warning about my speeding. Apparently they'd been following me because of a bad taillight.

The officers offered to give a hand with changing the tire. Nathaniel thanked them, but refused. He assured them, I'd give him a hand.

"Mr. Alexander is going to give me ride to the auto parts store," Nathaniel said.

I nodded my head in agreement and once the officers were out of earshot, I thanked Nathaniel for helping me dodge a bullet.

As we walked towards my car, Nathaniel whistled, "She sure is a beaut. Could I drive?" he asked.

"Sure," I said, "Just take it easy on the gas. She doesn't like to be driven hard."

The parts store was about three miles away, I tried to make small talk, but he was so fascinated with my car he paid me little attention.

When we approached our exit, I offered, "Nathaniel, slow down before you miss the exit."

He kept whistling and driving, as if I was the only one who saw the exit sign.

Then it hit me that I had been volunteered for more than a simple tire change. He ignored me like a yellow traffic light and continued on, cruising past exit after exit. I rested my head on the passenger window like a bored child in the back of a minivan.

"Tell me about your wife," he instructed. "She's what youngin's call a brick house."

"Excuse me?" He was a stranger, albeit a familiar one.

"I was only admiring the picture on your dash. Were you two newlyweds?" he asked in a respectful tone.

I felt a little embarrassed at almost having given him a piece of my mind. I took a deep breath and opened up.

"She's as beautiful as she was the first day I met her. After twenty-two years and two children, she still makes young girls get jealous with the curves she handles so well."

"Tell me about your family," he instructed.

"What do you want to know?" I asked.

He laughed. "Tell me how the two of you met."

I told Nathaniel how many years ago, when I was still in my teens, there was a radio station that broadcast local talent every Sunday morning. "Sunday Morning Glory" was the name of the show and hosted by a good friend of my father, named Mr. Edgars. The host usually opened the show with current local news, followed by showcasing local talent either before or after commercial breaks. If you got showcased the people in the community treated you like a celebrity. Because I was very familiar with all the bands and singing groups, I anticipated tuning into the show every Sunday before church waiting to hear if one if my friends would be on.

I told him about how my father would say, "A shiny shoe compliments a suit like pearls around a women's neck." So on the edge of the bed with shoe polish in hand I routinely sat, listening to the radio, as a I shined my and my father's hard-bottom shoes, and that on one particular Sunday I met my wife to be.

I told him how it felt as if she'd crept into my room like a skilled assassin and stole my heart. Her presence was so strong. Someone I hadn't even laid eyes on lured me in. I had no other choice but to cooperate with this ambush and waltz to the rhythm of her melody. I knew the very moment I heard her that I had to meet her.

After her song was done, the radio host went straight to commercial break. I hurried over to my room's door and locked it so my younger siblings wouldn't disturb me. I leaned in close to the radio, so close my ear was maybe an inch away from the speaker. I didn't want to miss any detailed information about her. I wanted more than just her name and age, I wanted to be her lover. I assumed she was new to town because talent like that doesn't go unnoticed in small towns, neither do pretty girls. "Tell Me about Jesus" was the name of the song she sang. She could convert an atheist just by how she sung the name Jesus.

"Man, that's powerful," Nathaniel said.

"Yes, sir, powerful enough to make me marry her." We both laughed.

I continued recounting our love story, telling him that it would be six months before I'd actually get to meet her. During those months, like a detective, I questioned people. No one knew, not even the boys in the neighborhood. I was too bashful to have straight talk with my dad about her so I asked him to ask Mr. Edgars if I could clean up around the station. Mr. Edgars agreed. The money wasn't much, but if that's what it took to find out more about my dream girl, I was willing.

Mr. Edgars was very kind and allowed me to do more and more work around the office. I mostly ran errands. I rarely got time to ask him anything about who would be the next feature artist on the show. Often I tried hinting around, asking Mr. Edgars casual questions, before slipping in my true intentions: questions about my dream girl. Mr. Edgars ignored me when I tried to get more details out of him.

For six long months I dreamt of her walking into the studio, singing as she walked the halls of the station. In this dream, I would bump into her and our eyes would lock. My dream didn't come true and after six months of waiting, I gave up and quit working at the station. Sweeping floors and fetching coffee wasn't that rewarding, plus, again, the pay wasn't that great.

"The things a man will do for a woman," I recalled.

"Amen!" Nathaniel said.

I went on to tell Nathaniel that my father had just bought me my first car. I needed a job that would pay at least what a full tank of gas was worth. After about a week into the school year, I noticed on the school bulletin that they were looking to hire student bus drivers. Being a bus driver wasn't the ideal job for someone who's concerned about impressing his peers but I applied for the job because cash was king. Two weeks later I was hired. The following week I was the ride-along, learning hands-on from a man named Mr. Bolden. He was a kind old man after school hours, but on the bus, Mr. Bolden acted as if the bus was a tank and he was the commander. I can still remember how afraid I was of him the first day Mr. Bolden picked me up for elementary school.

I told Nathaniel that my job was simple: stick to the route and make sure I delivered the students safely to school. Mr. Bolden had also advised me to separate work and play, and that I should socialize with my peers only after I'd delivered them safely. I memorized all twenty-three students, first and last names, within the first month. The job was more rewarding than I thought, and the buzz around school was that everyone wanted to ride my bus. I really didn't do anything special but open the door and greet everyone with a smile, but because everything was going so well, the route administrator added one additional stop to my route. Boy was I excited. I never thought my popularity at school would grow all because of driving the bus.

"Ok, Mr. Popular," said Nathaniel chuckling.

I continued, "It was Friday morning and I was feeling great. So great that I decided to clean up a little bit and throw on my favorite shirt and a little extra cologne, just enough cologne to be remembered. I had a lunch date planned with a young lady that I was pretty thrilled about. My plan was to ask her to the football game that night. As usual I delivered all my passengers safely to school. While walking to class it dawned on me that I forgot about the additional stop that was added to my route. I hurried to drop my books off to my classroom, then sprinted back to my bus. I didn't want to lose my job.

"I was so worried I wouldn't make it to my destination in time that I drove right past my stop, about 100 yards to be exact. I slammed on breaks and slid another thirty yards before coming to a complete stop. Slamming breaks on a dirt road wasn't the best idea. It looked like a landmine had gone off. Besides the fact that it was hard to see through the cloud of dirt, the strong scent of burning rubber and breaks made it hard to breathe. I put the bus in park and stepped out to see if there was anyone at the stop. I walked a few yards until I could see clearly and that's when I saw a young lady headed in my direction.

"I yelled, 'I need to turn the bus around, I'm coming to get you!' I hurried back to my bus, cranked it up, and put it in drive. Too embarrassed, I avoided eye contact as I slowly pulled the lever that opened the door. She stepped on the bus and said good morning in a soft tone, then she walked to the back to have a seat.

"Because she sat at the back of the bus I couldn't make out whether I knew her or not. She sat there quietly looking out the window as if she was dreaming of another place. The silence of the ride made things feel awkward for me, and it didn't help that she sat on the last seat at the back of the bus! A little reserved about pitching conversation, I turned on my little portable radio. I only used the little radio for two occasions, fishing and for the ride home after I dropped the students off. But now was a good moment to break the silence. The radio announcer says, 'Here's yours truly Sam Cook.' Before Sam could get well into the first verse of 'Darling you send me,' I turned the radio off. I didn't want her to feel as if I was trying to put the moves on her."

"Mr. Clifford Casanova! I like the ring of that," said Nathanial.

I smiled. "From the back of the bus she asked me, 'Why did you turn it off?' I could hear her making steps closer to the front and told her to have a seat, please, and that she wasn't supposed to move seats while I was driving the bus."

I smiled again at Nathaniel. "At this point my future wife said, 'I'm going to marry Sam Cooke one day.' I thought to myself, yeah, you and every other teenage girl, but I turned the radio back on and watched her through the rearview mirror as she reclined in her seat as if Sam himself was sitting next to her. After the song ended, she thanked me. She told me her father didn't let her listen to Sam Cooke since he'd crossed over to rhythm and blues."

I continued, "Out of habit I whistle when I run out of things to say, and to make light of things I figured I'd whistle a familiar hymn. If she knew anything thing about Sam Cook, besides his smooth olive skin and charismatic persona, she might give me a round of applause by the end of the tune or at least sober up and sit straight. In between whistling I snuck in a word or two just to let her know I could hold a tune. I looked in the rearview mirror to see if she enjoyed my chirping. Her head was down. I whistled on anyhow. Then, without warning, she stole the second verse from me and sang the chorus with holy conviction. Nathaniel, thank God I was at a stop sign, because I might of run off the road. She had more than a pretty voice. She had that thing that's hard to explain, but you know it's special because you can feel it. The old saints call that thing the anointing."

I shook my head at Nathaniel. "Man, oh, man, I had to grip the wheel so I wouldn't lose my cool. I didn't know who this young lady was but her voice touched me. It felt as if we'd kissed. She continued to sing as if the bus was filled with fans. Two miles from school, it hit me that I knew her. We were coming up on a four-way stop. I put the bus in park and stood up and faced her. I couldn't believe it was my dream gal! I stood mesmerized as if I was watching a magic trick. And then she yelled, 'Hey! What are you doing? Don't you hear those angry drivers blowing their horns at you?' I hurried and jumped back in the driver's seat and pulled off. Because I was so embarrassed I kept quiet for the remainder of the short drive, but that moment is when it all began."

"Beautiful story," said Nathaniel. "Isn't it funny how things work out?"

I enjoyed Nathaniel's company that day. What are the chances of me running into my counselor's assistant with a flat tire on the side of the road? Nathaniel seemed tired by the time we made it back to his car, and it had started to rain, but I didn't mind getting a little wet, if it meant being a Good Samaritan to my new friend.

Yeah it's been awhile
I hope heaven loves you
As much as I do,
Sweetness of mine.

I know they say a man ain't
Supposed to cry, but this pain
In my chest is rising
Straight to my eyes

The rainstorm turned to mist as the sun went down. I rolled my windows down, slightly reclined my seat, and counted streetlights as I cruised in the slow lane. Though the ride home was short, it was enough time to reflect on the day. The early morning kiss from my wife, the not-altogether-awful experience at my counselor's office, losing myself on backcountry roads, and changing Nathaniel's tire, ran through my mind with the same out-of-order ordering of movie scenes like most things did these days. The moist air felt different against my arm that hung out the driver's window. I had too much on my mind to be bothered.

I finally reached the light that would return me to my wife and daughter. I had the option to take the right towards home or take the left and revisit the place where things fell apart. I waited for the light to change. I hoped to change my mind about turning left. The cool air couldn't stop me from sweating. I was scared. I laid my head back against the headrest and took a few deep breaths to relax. My heart beat at a tempo too fast for my hands to clap. My mind fast-forwarded to what I perceived to be an outcome, and the outcome didn't make me relax at all.

Honk! Honk! Honk! A loud horn scared the hell out of me. At first I thought someone had rear-ended me. I turned to look over my shoulder and then realized there was a line of cars honking their horns and yelling for me to make a move. The man in the car behind me screamed out his window, "Green light!"

I pulled off so fast from the light I burned rubber. Though I turned left I could only hope and pray things turned out right. Not giving a darn about the speed limit, I raced ahead as if it was possible to run late to an old crime scene. This would be the first time that I drove down the same road of my son's accident.

I raced at eighty miles an hour on the dreary two-lane road. A mile up I saw a deer standing on the shoulder of the road. Because of the weather conditions, if he decided to cross to the other side, it was going to be hard to slow down and avoid the deer. I took my foot off the gas and gripped the steering wheel. I could see the deer flirting with the idea of crossing. This hesitation scared me even the more.

Ahead a huge oak tree ahead had boughs like gigantic biceps. I screamed when I saw the deer slowly step into the road. As I hit the break, I lost control. When I opened my eyes a few inches of cold air separated me from the oak. I frantically patted myself down, hoping my limbs still worked.

I pulled down the sun visor. I saw fear, which surprised me. I took a deep breath and exhaled slowly. I felt like the man watching me was calling me a coward, so I quickly opened my door. As I stepped from the car I noticed that a picture had fallen down from the visor.

It was a picture from Father's Day. I hadn't seen the photo in years. We were both dressed in our custom suits. My arms were placed around his shoulder as we posed in our most dapper ensemble. Looking at it brought back memories I wasn't sure I was ready to embrace. I can remember the sound and scent of the room that day. The cologne he wore was as strong as his young heart. Right before we took the picture, I had given him his first lesson on tying a tie. Surprisingly it didn't take long for him to get the hang of it. He often stood in my shadow and watched me shave and shine my shoes. The suits we wore were similar in color and design. He'd seemed happy to be next to me as I placed my arm around his shoulder and pulled him in close. As always, our hearts where woven together. At the count of three, I remembered we'd said, "Cheese."

After taking the picture I issued him a tall order, "Son! Make me a promise that someday you will teach your son how to tie a tie."

"Yes, sir," he replied with a smile.

I remember how I grabbed him with both arms and hugged him and kissed him on his forehead and told him that I loved him. I pressed the picture against my heart, wishing I could feel him again. From the glove compartment, I grabbed a small envelope and put the picture inside and hid it underneath the driver's seat.

Even though I knew exactly where I was, I felt like a refugee. To my right was a two-lane side street named Apple Valley. This road was used as a shortcut to avoid traffic lights. People tended to go fast or as slow as they wanted. There weren't any cars coming. My mind did what it came to do on this stretch of the road. I started to replay the accident as the eyewitnesses had described things.

I could hear the echo and feel the rumble of his motorcycle, as he rode in what I thought was my direction. I knew the ending by heart. What my son hadn't known was there was a car coming up behind him speeding. I screamed his name and signaled him to move out the way but I knew there was nothing I could do but let the story unfold.

I felt the impact as the car rammed his bike. I feel the pain as he was thrown from his motorcycle. His bike was dismantled, and he laid near it drifting in and out of consciousness, fighting for breath. I sat on the ground and pulled him into my arms. "Where is your helmet?" I ask. I sing his favorite song praying he'll join me in unison on the chorus. But I sing alone. When I open my eyes, he isn't there. Neither is there blood on my hands. It takes me a while to realize this was all a façade. Like a man in the desert who sees water, my thirsty heart longs to see my boy again.

I close my eyes tightly hoping just maybe I would get to see what happened before he turned down Apple Valley road. Thoughts of our last conversation flood my mind and leave me with regret. And this: Was I a good father? Was our relationship all it could have been? Is it my fault he died so young? Never in my life have I experienced something like this. It's like a living, recurring nightmare, but seeing something I never witnessed. I again visualize the details of my son's accident with clarity.

I quickly jumped up and dusted the gravel off my pants and ran to my car. I'd lost track of time again. I knew I needed to get home as fast as I could if I didn't want my wife to be worried. I made the thirty-minute trip in fifteen minutes. When I arrived home, I noticed something weird. The front door was wide open and all the lights were on. Smoke made its way out the front door like an unwelcomed guess.

I yelled her name and took a deep breath as I fought through the smoke like a shadow boxer.

"Where are you?" I screamed until I found my angel.

"Everything's okay. I'm in the kitchen," she answered calmly.

Once I knew she was safe, I held her tight, and rubbed my hands through her hair and we kissed.

"Sorry. I left the pot on the stove too long," she whispered in my ear. "How was your interview?"

"Interview?" I replied. I had forgotten that I told her I had an interview instead of the truth about seeing a counselor. Once I caught myself, I kissed her again and went on to brag about how well I'd done. To avoid being questioned any further I promised her we'd talk about it first thing in the morning.

"Let me sleep on it," I said then went to take a shower.

I turned the cold water on then sat down on the floor of the shower with my legs crossed and arms folded. My mind ran out of control, once again, like a film that had jumped the reel. I stayed there until I heard a knock on the door and my wife asking if I was okay.

The least of my problem was being clean. Simple things, like showing up for work were a drag. Other things, like putting on my work boots, felt like a chore. Even the distance from the front door to the car felt like a long incalculable journey. If I could, I would have left all of it behind, but I couldn't because my wife and daughter needed me.

When I arrived to work I did my best to avoid co-workers, especially Roy Morelli, the shortest, most talkative man I've ever known. I called him the Italian Stallion, because he swore he was God's gift to women. They say God protects babies and fools; Roy is both. There were several times I wondered why the company even hired him. His resume wasn't impressive. His work ethic barely average. I'd always told him that if his work ethic were even half as good as his jokes, his department's productivity would double.

Like a man who wore too much cologne, so was Roy to a workspace. He'd do anything to get a laugh, even if it meant embarrassing himself, but usually his off-brand of humor was at someone else's expense. There'd been a rumor circulating for years that our boss was homosexual. While I wasn't one for chin-wagging, it seemed pretty clear that this was, at the very least, a possibility. The gossip never crossed any line of respect. That is, until Roy catapulted over the it.

On our supervisor's birthday, Roy volunteered to coordinate a cake. Atop the cake had been a placard that read: Your secret is safe with us. When the song "YMCA" started to play and a male dancer came out, our boss tried to play it cool, but you could tell by the veins that bulged from his forehead that he was pissed. If it wasn't for my pleading on his behalf, Roy would have been fired.

On any given day, Roy was usually the second person I saw at work, but today there were no signs of him around, and no trace of his loud, booming voice that would, more often than not, be echoing in the hallway. Roy was responsible for scheduling my appointment with the counselor. Roy said he missed me laughing at his corny jokes. I agreed that if he scheduled an appointment I would go. Despite all evidence to the contrary, I trusted Roy. He didn't go into much detail, but to say he knew the counselor personally and could vouch for him.

I figured once he spotted me he'd hound me like a private investigator wanting details. Because of this, my plan was to skip lunch in order to avoid Roy, but, surprisingly, I was hungry. It helped that my favorite meal was being served: fried chicken, black-eyed peas, and cold sweet tea to top it off. The cooks were glad to see me. I didn't have to ask for an extra piece of chicken.

"The extra fat wouldn't hurt," said the chef.

"Thank you, sir," I replied as I pulled my sagging pants up on my waistline.

It was obvious I had lost some weight. This was the first time in weeks that I'd even stepped a foot near the cafeteria. To avoid my coworkers, I usually skipped lunch all together. Most days I'd sit in a restroom stall and cry, but today was different. Still I wanted to be alone, so I quickly grabbed my meal and went outside to eat. Though I ran into a few coworkers, they didn't say much, and I somehow managed to steer clear of Roy. There was an old tractor tire out back, a safe place to eat without being bothered. Little did I know that he was trailing me. Shortly after taking a seat on the ground and leaning back on the tire, I heard footprints. When I turned to look, because of the sun's glare, it was hard to determine who it was. Blue cargo pants and steel-toe boots all look the same from the waist down, regardless of who's wearing them.

"There won't be a starving ant a hundred miles east of the river!

There's enough butt crack here to eliminate hunger!"

I immediately jumped up to shake myself off. Around these parts, fire ants can be awful. The tingle of their venom lasts for days. Aggressively wiping myself down hoping not to get bit, my chicken toppled and I spilled my drink. Then it hit me. There were no ants. When I realized there were no ants, no sweet tea, and my chicken was covered in sand, I lunged forward and scooped Roy off his feet and wrestled him to the ground. I'm not sure what came over me, but this strange burst of adrenaline felt good. For a moment, I felt...I guess the word is alive, even if I looked ridiculous. What could be more embarrassing than two out-of-shape men in their mid-forties tussling like kids trying to prove their strength on a playground? Neither of us landed any serious blows, but I did put him in a headlock that I'm sure must have scared him a bit. I felt like a chronic smoker trying to run a 100-yard sprint, and I quickly ran out of breath. I tried stooping over to catch it, but it didn't work, and I had to lie down.

With what little breath I had left I shouted, "Man, you're crazy!"

"I'm sorry," he replied.

I could see he was just as tired as I was. I pointed my index finger right between his eyes and he stared into the bull's eye of mine. He was frozen by my fury. A part of me wanted to slap the prankster out of him. Instead I reached down, picked up a piece of chicken skin, and set it on top of Roy's head. Watching dirt and grease slide down his face satisfied my hunger for retaliation.

"I never had dirty chicken, Clifford, but with some dirty rice this might make a good meal," he said.

This was an obvious attempt to make me laugh. And, boy, did I. I laughed hard, so hard I couldn't control myself. It was the kind of laughter that could substitute a thousand crunches.

We walked back to the office. He didn't mention the appointment he'd made with the therapist. He didn't ask anything more than how my weekend had gone, and because of this I was reminded of the reason I considered Roy a friend.

"Everything is everything," I replied.

We shook hands and returned to our separate workspace. I quickly shut the door as soon as I walked into my office. With my back against the door I whispered a prayer so loudly that only God could hear. From the depths of my soul I prayed. *Dear God, I don't know how to feel about you, neither do I understand you, but please help me.*

Before I could complete my prayer, I was interrupted by a voice that said my name. The hair on the back of my neck stood up. I thought it was God audibly speaking. I stood still, pretending like I hadn't heard my name. If this was the voice of God, certainly he could see I was scared, and only pretending to be bold.

Bang! Bang! Bang!

"Hey, Clifford, are you in there?"

The voice sure wasn't God's.

"What do you want, man?" I called out as I returned a bang on the door.

"I know you're in there," he answered.

"What do you want, Roy?"

I looked up to God and gave him the frown from hell. When I opened the door, there was Roy, standing with the biggest smile ever.

"I know I messed up your lunch. I wanted to make it up to you," he said.

He handed me a hot plate of fried chicken, ice tea, and, surprisingly, a piece of cheesecake.

"It's the least I can do after ruining your lunch," he said.

I welcomed him in my office. I was less hungry at this point, but I ate, figuring the more I chowed down, the less we would talk. He sat with me as I ate in silence. When there was only my dessert left on the plate, he walked to the door, he paused and placed his hand on my shoulder and held his head down. He then closed his eyes and said a few words. I couldn't make it out, but I could feel the sincerity in his mumblings.

I told him that I'd made it to the counseling session and that I appreciated his recommendation.

He nodded, and then he said, "I'll leave you to your cake."

Bible study started at 7:30. It was about 7:15 before I even considered getting dressed. Being late wasn't my style. I despised tardiness. Because I often lead most of the devotional services I usually arrived extra early to make sure the PA system ran properly. Still, I had to beg myself to get dressed. Singing has always been my therapy, but my soul hurt so badly that it was all I could do to open my mouth to speak much less sing. I had lost my song, and my passion was dwindling faster and faster. I arrived late. Devotional services had started without me.

Being late was starting to become my new normal. After realizing this was the fourth week I'd been late, I said to myself, *Screw it!* and headed back to my car. I was too embarrassed to come up with another excuse. I thought I'd made it back to my car without being noticed, when I heard the pastor's voice yelling from across the parking lot.

"Brother Clifford!"

I was in no mood to talk but out of respect I turned and smiled and told him I was heading back to the car to grab my Bible. I couldn't believe I was lying to his face. I'm no liar. I was only trying to make an exit without being noticed. Pastors have a way asking indirect questions hoping to get beneath the surface. I was familiar with that technique, only because my dad was a pastor. I assumed he was just doing his job, checking up on the well being of the sheep.

"Brother Clifford, is everything okay?" he asked.

Tripping over my words because nothing was okay — and never again would be — and my tongue was tied, I replied with a simple yes. He complimented me, expressing what a strong and faithful man I was. Like hell I was...still I'd allow him this perception of me. He invited me to lunch the next day, but with yet another lie, I told him I was busy remodeling the house. Oftentimes churches fall short, forgetting people are more than parishioners and tithers, but humans trying to walk though the complexities of life, but he seemed sincere and asked my permission to pray with me. I agreed and we grabbed hands.

His words were: "When one weeps, we all weep. God open our eyes so we can see the pain of our brothers and sisters, Amen."

I did my absolute best to hold my tongue during my pastor's prayer. Maybe I was strong; it took strength to refrain from scream-ing at my pastor that our God was a vengeful, spiteful God. I con-sidered letting loose. Oh how I wanted to let loose. I had a thing or two to say about weeping and how I couldn't go an hour without having to find a place to cry and how no one in our congregation could say a damned thing about my pain, unless they'd lived it. Sure, God might have something to say; he'd lost a son. As for ev-eryone else, what did they know about the pain of losing a child. But who was I fooling? I stuck to my initial game plan, smiled the smile of a jaguar, and with a nod, hopped back in my car.

I had no destination in mind. Wherever the road took me was okay. Before pulling out of parking lot I laid my head back on the headrest and took a few deep breaths. With tears running down my cheek I sat up to take a look into the rearview mirror, so I could see what it looked like to see myself cry.

My fear, hurt, pain, and guilt played before me as if I were on a stage. This was real life, no hired actors and no special effects. Filled with despair, I drove until the car's dash light alerted me I was about to run out of gas. I pulled to the nearest exit to fill up. I reached into my pocket for cash to pay the clerk and realized I had the number to the counselor's office balled up in my pocket and the quarter Nathaniel had thrown me.

I sat at least an hour in the car rehearsing the conversation I'd planned on having with my counselor. I've made tough decisions in my life but making this phone call was difficult, maybe because my life was on the line.

After the first ring, I wanted to hang up. This doesn't make any sense. I thought to myself. After the third ring, the answering machine picked up. I gave it my best shot at sounding strong, saying my last name with confidence because I had something to prove. Halfway into my message I realized someone had picked up the phone.

"Clifford, is that you?"

"Who is this?" I asked.

"Clifford, is that you?" someone asked again.

Not understanding how someone knew my name, but I not recognize the voice, I asked the anonymous person to hold on while I reach into my pocket to make sure I dialed the right number and didn't call home by mistake.

"Clifford, it's me Nathaniel."

"I was calling to check on the next available time I could meet with the counselor. Would you mind taking my number down and leaving a message?" I asked kindly.

"No problem," said Nathaniel.

I gave him my office number because I didn't want my wife to know.

"You have dinner yet?" he asked.

"I don't think my wife would be too pleased to know I skipped one of her meals," I offered, but the truth was she hadn't cooked in a while. "But, no, I haven't. Did you have something in mind?"

"Dinner. My treat."

"What's the address?" I asked.

After we agreed to meet in twenty minutes. Cold hearts don't cook warm meals. Out of respect, and if I wanted home-cooked dinners the rest of the week, the least I could do was to call home and let my wife know my plans. I told myself to call home as soon as I made it to the restaurant.

I was familiar with its location and jetted over in hopes of arriving before Nathaniel. When I arrived I noticed a man dressed in all black standing at the door with his arms crossed. I assumed he was the host. He greeted me kindly with a big smile and a handshake. Because of his warm welcome it made it easy to ask for change for the pay phone. We joked briefly about being married and checking in with our wives, so he understood my dilemma.

He escorted me into the restaurant, took me to the office, and allowed me to use their personal phone.

"It will only take a second," I said.

"Take your time," he replied as he walked away.

I let the phone ring for a few but no one picked up. We didn't have an answering machine at home so I continued to hang up and call back until she answered. I figured if she didn't answer I'd better skip dinner and head home. Finally after the third attempt calling, she answered.

"Is everything okay?" I asked her.

I told her that I was meeting a buddy for dinner.

"I won't be long, a reasonable time, couple hours," I said.

"Take as long as you want, Clifford, but bring me some dessert home." She said this coyly, almost as if she were flirting, but she sounded exhausted.

"Absolutely," I replied, then we kissed the phone at the same time.

As I walked back to the front of the restaurant, I realized how overdressed I was. Even though my tie was undone and collar loosened, I still appeared a little uptight for this type of scene.

I thanked the host and told him I would be right back. I had an old pair of blue jeans and a T-shirt in the trunk that I could change into. This wasn't your five-star restaurant. It was more of a juke joint.

Because I walked out so fast I ignored the faces I felt looking my way, but I did notice a stage with instruments waiting to be played. After changing clothes in the parking lot, I sat and waited for Nathaniel to arrive. I stared at the building from the parking lot across the street, watching the kind of folks that walked in and also in hopes of spotting Nathaniel before he walked inside. Nathaniel arrived about five minutes later.

I remained in the car and watched closely as Nathaniel walked to the front of the building. Because this spot was his idea, I assumed he knew more about the place than just the taste of the food. He seemed very comfortable with the host, as I watched them dap each other up.

After the two chatted a good two minutes Nathaniel appeared to be scanning the parking lot for me. I flashed my headlights at him. He waved, signaling me to come over. He met me halfway as I crossed the street. He seemed excited to see me. Because Nathaniel is such a big, burly man, it felt like I was being bear hugged, as he wrapped his right arm around my shoulder.

"What's the deal with this spot?" I asked.

After all my years of living in this city, I thought I knew where all the soul food diners where.

"It's just a little hole in the wall. Good old country folk. You know, whisky, wine, and blues kind of folks. It's a good place to relax and have some fried chicken," he offered.

"Pretty nice spot," I said as I admired portraits on the wall.

Everyone was kind to Nathaniel. He was more than just a regular patron, but an admired person with a hero's persona. Everyone who greeted him greeted me with the same respect. I felt like batman's sidekick. With all the kindness shown, I felt connected to these people and the whisky that hid under each "Nice to meet you, Clifford." It felt good to be standing next to such a giant of a man.

"So what you think?" Nathaniel asked.

"I'm hungry," I replied.

He introduced me to our server. I took my hat off to greet her like a gentleman. She ignored my handshake and went straight for a hug and informed me that hugs and good food make a merry heart. She took our order and before I could get comfortable, our food was back on the table. Amen.

"Who are those guys walking in with the instruments?" I asked Nathaniel.

"That's the house band," he replied.

It was obvious these cats were musicians by the cool in their stride. They carried nonchalant confidence, as if they knew they were going to move the crowd.

"Tonight is open mic jam session. If you don't mind hanging out a little longer, I'm sure you will enjoy the talent," said Nathaniel.

"As much as I want to stay, it isn't a good idea for me to hang late."

"You sure?" he replied.

To keep from changing my mind, I went to the restroom. I stood at the sink and washed my hands repeatedly. I tried to justify my reason for wanting to stay, but I couldn't fool the man in the mirror. I could hear the band warming up. The groove of the bass line started my foot tapping. This wasn't no DJ, this was live music. I could feel the kick drum and bass vibrating through the walls as if they were playing right in front of the bathroom door. A guest interrupted me.

"Excuse me, sir," I said as I slid over to the urinal.

"It's going to be a great night," guy said.

"Why is that?" I asked.

"They're some super bad singers and musicians in the house tonight."

I walked out the restroom and stood in the corner of the room. I couldn't believe what I was hearing. I noticed our waitress a few feet away from me. I asked her if she minded if I used the phone. I knew if my wife heard the music, she wouldn't mind me staying out a few extra hours. I was amazed at what I was hearing. I hid in the corner like a talent scout watching the exchange of energy between the performer and audience; these musicians were connected with the crowd.

To my surprise Nathaniel was the master of ceremony. Nathaniel handled the crowd like an expert, telling a few jokes, making the people laugh. He was a natural.

"Ladies and gentlemen, we have a special guest in the house tonight, so put your hand together for my good friend, Mr. Clifford."

The audience clapped as if they had been waiting all night for this. I was anxious to see the grand entrance. Nathaniel raised his hand high and signaled for me to walk towards him, and I did, only because I thought he needed help with something. About halfway to the stage Nathaniel says, "Give it up one more time for Mr. Clifford."

I didn't have a clue he was talking about me getting on stage until he stooped down and whispered, "What song you like to sing?"

Each step toward the stage felt like I was walking in mud. The anxiety was overwhelming. Nathaniel met me at the corner of the stage and pulled me up. He smiled and I stared back in unbelief.

"What song would you like to sing?" he asked again.

I leaned in close to remind him I was only here to eat, not sing. Over the years I've learned how to make arguing on stage look like banter. It was too late to turn around now; I was too committed to coward out. I turned to the band and told them to put me in the key of A major. The guitar player and pianist both played an A major chord. This wasn't a band of rookies. I looked over my shoulder and the band was at full attention waiting on my command. I stepped into the spotlight and grabbed the mic like it was my first time. I tapped the mic.

"Testing one, testing two."

The mic squealed just a little. Luckily the stage lights were bright and prevented me from seeing the eyes in the audience, but I did hear chatter, anxious ears waiting for the first note.

"How's everyone doing this evening? I wasn't expecting to sing tonight, but my good friend Nathaniel suggested I do a song."

The audience cheered me on. I turned and sarcastically smiled at Nathaniel. Boy, was I nervous. My hands were sweaty, so sweaty I could probably wash a dish.

"Does anyone like Sam Cooke?" I asked the middle age crowd. I heard only a few claps. I thought maybe they weren't impressed.

One guy yells from the crowd, "Come on, man, sing. We don't have all night."

It was hard to identify who was talking, the man or the whisky.

"Just don't throw tomatoes at me," I said jokingly, and the crowd laughed.

I counted the band in at the tempo of a slow shuffle Ballard and begun to sing.

If you ever, change your mind

About leaving, leaving me behind.

Girl, bring it to me, bring your sweet loving

And bring it on home to me.

Before I started to sing the second verse there were couples slow dancing with the look of love in their eyes, as the melody moved them gently from left to right. Cupid was now in the building and I was supplying him with arrows. The band continued to play after I finished the last verse to preserve the mood. The mood was set for whoever was coming behind me. I tried to sneak off the stage, but Nathaniel insisted that I sing another tune.

"The people love it," he said.

I encouraged the crowd to keep slow dancing like no one's watching. I turned around to the band and quickly hummed out the groove of the next song. They were on it! We transitioned smoothly.

Cupid draw back your bow and let your arrow go

Straight to my lovers heart for me

Cupid please hears my cry and let your arrow fly

Straight to my lovers heart for me.

Not only were the customers up dancing but the employees were two-stepping from table to table, serving and taking orders. *That's the meaning of soul food,* I thought to myself as I watched what was happening.

After finishing the song, the audience was kind to give me a standing ovation, even though the majority of them were already standing. The soundman turned the house lights on, and I could really see all the radiant smiles shining my way. Feeling overwhelmed with joy, I hugged Nathaniel with open arms and thanked him. He grabbed my hand and raised it, like I was a champion.

We both walked off stage together and immediately the people surrounded me as if I were a celebrity. Some asked if I was a recording artist and a few asked for an autograph. I signed at least thirty napkins. I considered myself a good singer but not good enough to give someone my signature. But they insisted, so I signed away. It felt good to be appreciated.

I decided to stick around and listen to some of the local talent and, boy, was I impressed. I thought I was good, but these cats were great! I sat next to Nathaniel in awe. I leaned over to Nathaniel and asked why these amazing performers were still playing small clubs, when they had big stage potential.

"These aren't locals, these singers and musicians perform all over the world," he said. "The reason they come back to perform is the same reason college kids go home on the weekend: to get a home-cooked meal. They also pay respect to the place where they got their start. This is a mecca for musicians," Nathaniel said.

He educated me on the history of this cool restaurant. At first when I walked in, I noticed the nice art and pictures on the wall, but I didn't know they had any significance. With all the icons on the wall, I felt like I was sitting in the presence of gods and they were evaluating my performance!

As much as I really wanted to stay an extra hour, my time was coming to an end. I thanked Nathaniel for his kindness and hoped to return the favor one day. I walked to my car a little different then when I walked in. There was pep in my step, and my esteem was high! I even whistled and walked to the tempo of the last groove. Even the drive home was pleasant.

That night I enjoyed some of the best sleep I'd had in a long time. Not once was I awakened by a nightmare. I hibernated through the night and was peacefully woken by the sun.

"Good morning, sleeping beauty," was the first thing I heard, followed by a kiss on the cheek.

My eyelids were still glued shut, but the voice I knew all to well.

"How's daddy's girl?" I asked.

She hugged me as if she knew my arms would never fail her. I hugged her tightly, holding on to the only child I had left.

"Never have I known you to not be the first person awake," she said.

She continued on reminding me what it was like growing up with me: the 7am wakeup shrugs and loud, thunderous walking around the house before sun came up. We laughed together and then I reminded her that things change.

"Well, as long as your love doesn't change towards me," she said.

"Of course not, sweetheart, I loved you before I saw your face. Now go and help your mother finish cooking breakfast."

Before doing anything else of importance, I kneeled down just to tell God thank you for hugging me this morning. After a brief conversation with God I walked over to my window and stared into the sky, hoping my son would appear from behind the clouds and ask me to play catch.

I slowly backed away from the window and laid down on the bed and wept loudly with my mouth closed. Tears filled my ears. I grabbed my pillow to muffle my groan, so no one would hear me. I knew my daughter was behind the door weeping with me. She did her best to go unheard, but every parent knows the sound of their child crying.

I quickly jumped up and peeked through the crack of the room door and saw her there laying in a fetal position weeping. I eased down to the floor and reached my hand through the crack and rubbed her head. No explanation needed, we know there was a hole in our hearts that no amount of time could heal. The macho man in me wouldn't allow me to cry long, there was family breakfast waiting on us.

Because we both loved singing, I started singing the melody to one of her favorite songs. We looked into each other's eyes and sang to each other of our broken hearts. Before long we were both on our feet dancing together like it was our last dance at the prom. At that moment, I saw my daughter as a little girl. The feelings of thankfulness overwhelmed me, so we continued to dance until being interrupted by my wife. She surprised us by singing the third part harmony. I tossed my wife and daughter the remote control and hairbrush. They used them as their microphones. I grabbed the coat rack and pretended to play the upright bass.

We were having so much fun we forgot about our empty stomachs. It wouldn't be long before the bacon started to burn. The smoke alarm went off and it sounded like fireworks downstairs. We raced downstairs. My wife was the first one to make it to the kitchen.

"Dear God, we thank you for all you have done in our lives. We also thank you for this season of life that we are in. Pain has ripped us apart but love keeps drawing us together. Thank you for the food and all of your many blessing."

The doorbell rang, immediately followed by knocks on the door.

I assumed it was local missionaries, but the knocks on the door sounded personal. Because I was starving I ignored the knocks and sat down and started eating.

"Honey, sit down. Let's enjoy the burnt bacon."

She asked me to at least peek out the window. I declined and held my orange juice in the air and made a toast.

"Cheers!"

The knocking continued.

"I hope it's Ed McMahon with a $100,000 check," I said laughingly.

"Well, I hope it's a vacuum cleaner salesman," she replied with a wink.

The knocking aggravated her more than me, so she went to see who was at the door.

"Clifford, there's a man at the door to see you."

"Is it important?" I yelled from the kitchen.

"Clifford, you need to come here and get the door," she demanded.

I grabbed a slice of bacon and bread.

"This better be worth it," I mumbled with a mouthful of food.

I exaggerated my steps on the hardwood floors, hoping to sound disturbed. Before making my presence known, I hid behind the wall near the front door, trying to see who it was. It wasn't long before I recognized the deep Southern accent. It was Nathaniel. I was glad to see his face, but also curious.

"What brings you — ?"

He handed me my driver's license.

"I thought you might need this before starting your day," he said, sounding like my father.

Margaret announced the fact that losing things like keys, wallets, and even my driver's license was normal behavior for me.

"Hi, I'm Margaret. I've told him a thousand times to keep his license in his wallet but he insists on keeping it in his pant's pocket."

"Well, our waitress found it on the floor near our table," Nathaniel offered.

I laughed, even though my wife didn't think it was that funny, and welcomed him to join us for breakfast. Nathaniel accepted. While escorting him to the living room, I bragged about my wife's cooking, as if her cooking was second to none.

"Have you ever heard of Frank's Diner?" I asked Nathaniel.

"I've never been, but I heard their food was good for the soul," said Nathaniel.

"Well, you're in for a treat!" I leaned over to Nathaniel and whispered to him that my wife, years ago, was one of the original cooks at Frank's.

To make Nathaniel feel welcome, we served him as if he'd been invited. We chatted for a while before being summoned to the kitchen by my wife. Once we were all gathered at the breakfast table, we grabbed hands, as I blessed the food.

"Dear, Lord we give thanks to you again. We thank you for giving us this day and daily bread. Thank you for Nathaniel and bless him for returning my belongings. Like a dog bringing a bone to his master, so did Nathaniel bring me my license back, Lord. So Lord, bless him with a treat."

My wife didn't find my humor appropriate. She squeezed my hand as hard as she could but my left foot paid the price.

"Ouch and Amen!" I yelped.

Nathaniel chuckled. I think he knew my wife was throwing blows under the table all while keeping her face in the direction of our guest. It's rude to argue in the presence of company, so I kissed my wife and whispered sweet nothings in her ear.

Because my daughter, Connie, is a social butterfly she didn't hesitate asking Nathaniel all sorts of questions. To keep my family from knowing the complete truth about who Nathaniel was, I answered for him. Giving them very little details on how we met and the nice dinner we had had.

"Be quite! Clifford, let Nathaniel speak for himself," said my wife.

He somehow knew the predicament I was in. Maybe the helpless look in my eyes, suggested that he smile a lot and talk very little. He tapped my foot beneath the table and carried on conversation like a pre-rehearsed script. Before we knew it Nathaniel had us laughing. Even my wife let down her hair. I caught her laughing with food in her mouth. I'd be a fool if I'd brought that to her attention.

We continued to enjoy Nathaniel's company, but because I wanted some one-on-one time with Nathaniel, I asked my wife if she'd mind if I showed him my music collection. Whenever I mentioned my music collection, she'd usually allow me to escape the drudgery of washing dishes.

"Make yourself at home," I said as I open the door to my man cave.

I walked over to my record player and put on some old timey gospel music. I was certain that we were both grounded in the same musical soil. Good music makes for good conversation. For the first ten minutes the album did more talking than we did until Nathanial stopped the music.

"What was all of that about?" he asked.

"I guess it's time for confession," I replied.

He nodded in agreement. Clearly I had more on my mind than listening to old records. Despite being embarrassed, I held my head up and confessed that no one, not even my wife knew I had sought counseling. Even the closest of my friends bought into the wall I put up, disguised as strength, pain concealed by a painted smile.

"I felt some wall was about to break," I told Nathaniel.

He remained quiet, as I continued exposing my heart.

"Just an hour ago my daughter caught me crying. Many nights I console my wife but deep down I know I needed consoling."

While talking to Nathaniel, I couldn't sit still. My emotions held me at gunpoint and left me contemplating ways of escaping confrontation without getting hurt. Nathaniel wasn't a counselor. He was barely a friend, but I felt he understood exactly where I was coming from. After blabbering for a good fifteen minutes I apologized to Nathaniel for holding him hostage with my personal grief.

He stood up and slowly walked around the room and stared at the pictures and plaques on the wall. He remained quite in his observation. I assumed he was impressed by some of my achievements.

My personality was plastered on the walls in the form of accolades, which made it obvious the kind of man I am. I excused myself from the room to go check on my wife. Nathaniel was trustworthy, so I felt comfortable leaving him alone in my personal space.

"Can I bring you a Pepsi?" I asked.

"Sure," he replied.

I remembered my first time at the counselor's office, Nathaniel gave me water in a mason jar. I thought he might think it was funny if I handed him soda in a mason jar. I asked my wife where we kept the mason jars. She ignored me, found mason jars, and poured two Pepsis.

While walking back to where Nathaniel was, I felt this uncontrollable urge to laugh, which made it difficult to walk while holding two drinks. I giggled all the way back to the room. I couldn't wait to see the look on Nathaniel face once I handed him his drink.

The door to my man cave was barely open. I stood at the door hoping Nathaniel would hear me. I used my foot to tap on the door.

"Nathaniel give me a hand!"

I waited for his response. I heard nothing. My initial thought: I hope the old man wasn't dead, but then again he did have bad hearing. Because the door was slightly cracked, I was able to pull the door open with my foot. I wish I'd kept the door closed because

I wasn't prepared to deal with what I was about to see.

I dropped the drinks. The sound of shattering glass alarmed him. I reached over to grab his shoulder.

"What the hell are you doing? Who told you to snoop through my belongings?" I was furious.

I demanded he go. Nathaniel didn't resist leaving, neither did he explain.

"He's a wise old man," I said underneath my breath. I slammed the door so hard I dropped the frame I was holding in my hand. It shattered and that made me even angrier. I even kicked the shattered glass around. I knew it wouldn't be long before my wife would come downstairs. I quickly cleaned up the mess and prepared myself to tell a lie if necessary to avoid further questioning.

While sweeping up the shattered glass, I noticed that Nathaniel left something behind. It was a courtesy card from the counselor's office requesting another appointment. At that moment I made up my mind to forget about the counseling sessions and declare war against my agony and leave it up to fate to decide who would win. I was about to rip the card in half until I noticed my wife standing at the door with both arms folded.

"Hey! Just doing a little cleaning," I said sarcastically.

"What happened?" she asked.

I lied and told her the hinges on the door needed fixing and that caused the picture frame to fall and shatter. I told a second lie that Nathaniel was running late for an appointment. To avoid any more questioning I told my wife how much Nathaniel enjoyed her cooking. She smiled and expressed how much she enjoyed his company.

"He's a wise old man," I said.

I promised her that I would wash the dishes. In return she blew me a kiss and went about her normal routines. I re-read the card Nathaniel left, and then put the card in my wallet. There was unfinished business with Nathaniel.

The day was still young but the Southern heat wasn't. I could use a workout to burn off those breakfast calories. There was an acre of grass and hedges needing to be cut. My yard looked like a jungle. Two weeks without maintenance and the grass tickled your knees. As much as I enjoyed my riding lawnmower, I was in the mood to use the push mower. I wanted to sweat. I hadn't use the push mower in quite some time. It was hidden under the house, tucked away as a friendly reminder of what hard work was. That mower was at least thirty years old.

Occasionally I used it as a tool for disciplining the kids when they were younger. The wheels squeaked and squalled as I pushed the mower onto the driveway. I sprayed a WD40 on the rusted screws that held the wheels together and filled the empty tank with gasoline. After priming the pump, I yanked the pulley, but it didn't give, not even a little. My shoulder started throbbing.

I had forgotten that the lawn mower was almost as old as me. It was the same mower I used when I was trying to make an honest buck as a kid. I tried a few more times to crank the mower, but it failed to start. I turned the mower over to check the blade and discovered old grass prevented the blade from turning. After

I removed the dark earthen mass, I pulled again, and this time the mower sounded like a slow starting train as it struggled to exhale.

Mowing reminded me of Saturday mornings. It was expected for me to be the first one awake every day, but even more so on the weekends. In order to beat the Southern heat you had to wake up before sunrise, especially if you planned on doing yard work. It was impossible to win at playing hide and seek with the sun. Even the shaded tree with all its branches couldn't protect you from being tagged by the sun. I once saw a bird running from the heat.

Junior hated waking up early on Saturdays; he despised it. Still I felt it was priority to teach him to work with his hands and sweat. He knew waking up on a Saturday meant cutting grass, washing cars, and running errands for his mother, which usually took up the majority of the day. Because waking up on Saturdays was hard for him, occasionally I'd let him sleep in just for a little while, until I had all the lawn equipment gassed up and ready. To wake him I'd crank the lawn mower and let it run right by his bedroom window. The lawn mower was old and loud, the perfect alarm clock for an eleven-year-old who's accustomed to listening to loud funk music. If the lawn mower didn't wake him I would throw pinecones at his window and if that didn't work, I'd walk back inside the house and pull the covers off him and tickle him until it hurt.

One morning he surprised me. As usual I let the lawnmower run loudly at his bedroom window. I even threw pinecones, but he didn't so much as peek out the window. As soon as I turned around to head back into the house, I was hit with a pinecone. Not just one, he had a bagful and I was being ambushed. I ran and hid behind trees to keep from being hit, but boy was he accurate at pegging me right in the chest. He didn't miss even though I was a moving target.

To make the best of the moment, I quickly gathered as many pine cones as I could and started throwing them back at him. I can still hear the sound of his young voice, "You can't hit, what you can't see," he said as he did a somersault and hid behind the nearest tree. I goaded him to continue throwing them at me. My way of winning the battle would be easy. The more he threw, the more he would have to rake up while I sat back and drank Kool-Aid in the shade. Every time I was hit, I moaned and groaned and pretended to be weakened by his attack.

I quickly ran around to the backyard and hid in the bushes. Behind the bushes was the water hose. I got ready to water him and the grass at the same time. I could hear his footsteps getting closer. He slowly tiptoed around the bushes, trying to go unheard. It didn't matter how silently he tried to step. Even the lightest steps wouldn't go unheard on the tall grass. I could see his little legs getting closer to the bushes. When he leaned over and peeked in the bushes, that's when I jumped out. All I heard was loud screams.

"Clifford!"

By the sound of the high-pitched voice, I knew I'd messed up. I dropped the hose in disbelief. There was my wife standing soaked. Besides her clothes being wet, her new hairstyle was destroyed. A thousand sweet kisses and "baby, I'm sorry" didn't mean a thing to a woman whose hair was destroyed because of you. I tried to blame my son, which was another mistake. I got down on my knees and tried to bargain with her, offering to do the dishes for the next month. But that wasn't good enough.

Before I could stand up and offer my wife a hug, I was struck in the back with an acorn. Junior threw an acorn at me, while in the middle of trying to reconcile with his mother. The fun battle was over, and I was serious, so serious that I turned around and demanded him to come to me. He walked towards me slowly with his head down. I looked at this as an opportunity to teach him, when to play and how to stay in his place as a child. But his mother saw things differently.

While facing Junior, I didn't know my wife had picked up the water hose.

"Make one wrong step," she said with the hose inches away from my ear.

I tried to be clever by ducking to avoid being hit but I slipped and fell. She proved she was a woman of her word and sprayed me good. Junior was a few feet away, laughing at me. I grabbed him, and pulled him to the ground with me.

"Laugh now," I said, as I tried to use him as a shield. But that didn't stop her from spraying. We were covered in mud and debris, which made it hard to see. I picked Junior up and ran from her but only made it a few yards before Junior slipped from my grasp and ran back to his mother. She giggled and threw her head towards our neighbors peeking through their blinds.

"Oh we have company," she said.

I had thought, why not give them something to gossip about. I took my shirt off and walked slowly towards her in a seductive way. I ran my fingers through her wet hair and kissed her passionately. Her red lipstick smeared all over my lips and cheeks then I grabbed my wife's hand, she twirled around, and we took a bow in our neighbor's general direction.

An exasperated Junior had shaken his head and said, "That's gross, but do it again 'cause they're still looking."

CHORUS

I planted lilies for you,
Paid them to the angels
When the day comes my life is through,
I can be with you

Why are things I have
The things I hate?
Gotta get rid of these demons
Help me release the weight

I hadn't talked to my father since the funeral. He could be very mouthy, overbearing, and insensitive at times, and it would be impossible to avoid him for long. I often stopped by my parent's house when I knew my father wouldn't be home, hoping to catch my mother on the front porch relaxing in her rocking chair. Her company was all I needed. It was late Monday when my sister called, demanding I call our father. I decided I'd wake early the next morning to join him at the lake. He always said Tuesdays were his Saturdays in that he preached Sundays, Mondays he was busy at the church office knocking out whatever fire had started burning on Sunday. That and he'd be fishing. He didn't talk much when he fished, so it was the perfect time for him to listen.

I knew if I made it to the lake by sunrise he would be on the edge of the banks reclined in his folding chair waiting for hungry bass. There was about a fifty-yard walk through the woods just to get to the banks were he fished. He knew that trail all too well, and didn't need the sun to see his way. Then again my father was the type of man who carried a Swiss blade Monday through Saturday. He exchanged the blade for the Bible on Sundays. He could slice you on Saturday and spit holy fire on Sunday, in other words, woe to the man who's sitting in his fishing spot before he gets there.

My father really enjoyed eating sardines and saltine crackers while fishing. I remember as a kid thinking, *Why eat fish while trying to catch fish?* It never made any sense to me. He called it "old man's ice cream." I stopped by the bait shop to pick up some bait and some "old man ice cream" for him, even though I knew he never fished without his snack.

The owner was behind the register. It had been a while since I had last seen him. A white gentleman with wrinkled hands the size of a fishnet, a true fisherman's hand.

"Good morning, Clifford," he said with a smile.

He went on to mention that my father had been here earlier. I wasn't in the mood to carry on a lengthy conversation so I replied with a short good morning. He was known for holding you hostage with old folklore fishing stories. Because I was the only customer in the store at the time, he felt obligated to educate me on the newest reel and bait. Not trying to be rude, I interrupted him by asking for the total.

"Sixty-seven dollars," he replied.

While reaching into my pocket, he kindly refused my payment. Initially I assumed he added my bill to my father's credit. My father did have a great reputation at the bait shop. My father, along with the owner often went on deep sea fishing trips. The old man removed his ball cap and placed it over his heart. Fishing hooks held the seams of his vintage ball cap together. He reached down behind the counter and pulled up a package and placed it in my bag.

I had no clue what he'd put in my bag. The look in his eye seemed sincere.

"Thank you, Mr. Thomas," I replied and shook his huge hands.

"No problem," he replied with his deep Southern accent.

I walked to my car feeling pretty good. Often fisherman gave away fish out of their abundance as a token of kindness to young, amateur fisherman. Mr. Thomas was raised during an era when men literally hunted and fished to provide for their families.

After arriving at the lake, I sat in my car for a few minutes and asked myself, what I considered whether I was ready to talk to my father and secondly how I'd respond if we saw thing differently.

We had a strange relationship. Often we stared face to face, but rarely did we see eye to eye. He was a handsome, dapper man, and I was reminded regularly by his female associates how blessed I was. There were traits that we shared, that I despised. Talking to him sometimes was like arguing with myself in the mirror. But that was my father, and I loved and respected him greatly.

There he was listening to sermons on his portable radio, having revival on the river and relaxing on his favorite rock. If he hadn't caught any fish within the first hour, he would petition Jesus for fishing strategies.

"Pass me the bait," were the first words I heard from his mouth.

He didn't even look my way, as I passed him the bait. He had an intense look on his face, as if he could see through the water and maneuver the bait directly into the fish's mouth.

"Your singing is going to scare away all the fish, boy," he said as he threw the reel back into the water. "Even your cologne is loud."

I pretended to laugh, but silently prayed and asked Jesus to feed the fish with my dad's bait. I took out my fishing rod and sat next to him. Sitting with him was nostalgic, bringing back moments of us fishing together when I was a young boy. My father teaching me how to bait and unhook a fish for the first time were experiences that I would never forget.

"I've been out here for an hour and haven't got a bite yet," he said with frustration. "What brings you out?"

"Looking for you," I said.

It wouldn't be long before he'd start sharing what he planned on preaching on Sunday. His sermons had titles like: "Fish for Jesus," "Step in the Water," "Jesus on the Boat," and "Water on the Word."

Only a man sitting on the river with a Bible next to his tackle box could conjure up sermon titles like that. For many years he was a postal worker. During those years his sermons had titles like, "Mail from Heaven," "Satan, You Got the Wrong Address," and my favorite, "Mailman Made My Morning."

I wasn't in the mood to hear the preacher. I wanted to hear words from my father's heart. One thing that inspired good conversation between us was baseball. Every Saturday morning, there was a local sports broadcast that would re-broadcast baseball games from the previous week. My father grew up during the Jackie Robinson era of baseball, what he called "the black sheep of the white pasture." He was a hero among blacks, so naturally he was role model to every young black kid, inspiring us to pick up a bat and ball.

About four innings into the baseball game the young and promising right fielder, Reggie Jackson hit a home run. We celebrated as if we were at the game, throwing our hats in the air and jumping around. We were so engaged in the game that we didn't notice that there was a fish yanking my father's rod so hard that his rod looked as if it was about to break.

"Help your old man," my father said, using all his strength to reel in the sea monster. I laughed on the inside as I watch him struggle.

After a long twenty-minute tug-of-war, my dad won. He was exhausted, so exhausted that he had to lie back on the ground just to catch his breath. The sea monster lay there exhausted too, with half his body in the water and the other half on the bank. My father asked me to pull the fish in, so I did.

This was the biggest fish I'd ever seen. There was going to be a lot of bragging going on later that evening. I must admit I was a little nervous dragging the fish out the water. I tided a rope through the fish's gills and hung it on a tree like a punching bag. My father had a tape measure in his tackle box. We had no way of weighing the seventy-two-inch striper bass. We could only guess the fish weighed at least half the weight of an adult man. My pops reached in his tackle box and grabbed his camera and took a picture of me standing next to the prize.

"Your uncles are never going to believe this," he said as he threw me the camera.

I took a few pictures of him hugging his catch. I assumed after catching the biggest fish in his life, he'd want to call it a day. But, instead, he left the sea monster hanging on the tree like a cherished ornament and picked up his rod, baited it, and cast it.

"So what's on your mind?" he asked.

Initially I was shocked by his question. I'd assumed he had a solution prepared before hearing about the problem. Because my dad was a pastor, he felt that God gave him insight into people lives, especially his kids. I blurted that I went to see a counselor.

"I see you like wasting your money," he replied.

My father wasn't a big supporter of secular opinions. He believe that spirituality was the solution to every problem, especially relationship problems. He has a "pray hard until the problem is fixed" type of philosophy.

As expected he preached a mini-sermon blaming my lack of leadership as the root cause for the problems in my life. He looked at me suspiciously and asked if I was paying my tithes to God. Because it was common practice for pastors to have access to the church's financial records, I knew he couldn't resist the temptation of asking me directly since I was no longer a member of his church. I remained quiet and just listened, hoping God might guide him on what to say.

"Sir, I didn't wake up at the crack of dawn just to come watch you fish, nor to be questioned about my relationship with God. The reason I'm here was to see you is that I've been depressed."

He was anxious to respond, so anxious that I noticed his fingers typing out yet another mini-sermon on his thigh. It was clear that he felt insulted. I asked him to listen without responding until I finished talking. He then relaxed and listened as I continued to pour out my heart. I talked for about ten minutes. I talked until I had nothing more to say. We both stared, looking into the water as if a message in a bottle would come floating to the banks with the answers to life. My father took a few deep breaths before responding. The anxiety became so overwhelming that I stood up.

"Do you remember the conversation we had about six months ago?" he asked.

I wasn't expecting to revisit a conversation that was almost a year old.

"Think harder," he said after noticing the confused look on my face.

My father often confused the difference of a conversation and a sermon so, initially I thought about the sermons he'd preached. It didn't take long before I gave up and asked him to refresh my memory. I was starting to grow impatient and because the weather was warming up, I began losing my cool.

"Do you remember stopping by the house and helping me wash my old truck?" he asked.

"Of course I remember!"

It had been years since he washed that old Ford truck, but anything other than small talk, I told him I couldn't recall. I recalled smearing the word "April" on the passenger side window and that the rust from the door panel smeared on my khaki pants.

"Is that all you remember?" he asked.

"Well, I do remember helping you wash the truck and chatting a little about baseball." I dug as deep as I possibly could, trying to recall the significance of one conversation, and then it hit me.

"Are you saying it's my fault?" I asked angrily, throwing my hat down. I demanded he explain himself.

He remained calm and sat still, ignoring my hostility, which provoked me to become angrier. Never in my life had I ever disrespected my father but now would be the time that I drew the line in the sand. I called him by his first name.

"Paul," I said loudly, so loudly that his name echoed down the river.

He turned and looked at me as if I was still that teenager who came home late after curfew. He stood, and we faced each other like two boxers at a title match, and the title of father and son was on the line. If his answer wasn't good enough for my heart he was going to lose his title as father in life.

"I know you're mad, but you have to face the truth," he said without any signs of compassion or empathy on his face.

With my fist clinched tight, for a brief second I considered punching my father. But thoughts of my mother kept me from striking him. She was always his saving grace. I've never cried in front of my father before but I couldn't hold back. It was harder to hold back from striking him, so I let the tears flow instead.

He pulled out a napkin to wipe my face, all while proving his point and blaming me for my son's death. I shoved his hand away from my face and pointed at him as if his head was the target. I didn't say one word! I packed up my belongings and walked away.

As I was walking, he called me by my first name. By the tone of his voice I could sense he still believed he was right and I was guilty. I threw up my hands in disgust and continued to walk back to my car. With each step my heart pounded loudly in my ears, so loudly that I could hear the beat of my heart.

I never understood how your heart could continue to pump blood while experiencing and feeling the pain of a broken heart in your chest. I thought the walk back to my car would give me time to calm down and sort through my anger. But the anger continued to build. When I noticed my father's truck I walked up and kicked it. The truck was old and beat up, so an extra dent would likely go unnoticed.

"How could he be so insensitive?" I asked myself aloud with my head on the steering wheel.

I thought after a few minutes, that my father would appear at the driver's side window begging for my forgiveness. But the reality was, he would rather stay at the river hoping to catch a fish. I hoped my father would be more of a guide and a help in the time of trouble, but that was wishful thinking on my part. Dads should be there when you fall off your bike and also when life fails you. You never grow too masculine or too old to receive a helping hand from your dad. It amazed me how a person could love someone they don't respect.

I suddenly though of Nathaniel. I hadn't decided whether or not I would go back to the counselor, but the last time Nathaniel and I talked, we'd left on bad terms. I knew I had overreacted. I also knew I owed him an apology.

Tuesday night was Bible study and my plan was to skip it like gym class and track down Nathaniel at the diner. I called home anyways and mentioned to her that I may miss Bible study class. Surprisingly, she didn't ask why. After hanging up, I sat back in my office chair and thought of extra things I could do around the office to kill time. By this time of the evening, it was me and the janitors left.

Because I had some time to kill, I asked Moses, one of the janitors, if he wouldn't mind me helping him mop. Moses was the oldest working employee. He possessed the optimism of a twelve-year-old, and, like an old newspaper, the tint of his skin advertised his age. He was one of the first African American employees the company hired after segregation. We all respected Moses and often we went to him for advice even though his advice could be harsh at times, we respected his honesty.

"You don't need four hands to mop, these two works just fine," said Moses.

Just the type of response I expected, sharp and militant.

"Are you sure, Mr. Moses?"

He stopped mopping and just stared at me, as if I was confused. He took steps towards me and reached out to shake my hand. Not once did he blink or smile which made me nervous. His firm grip immediately led me to think this was his way of proving his strength. His grip got tighter. I could hear my joints cracking.

"How's everything going, Mr. Clifford?" Moses asked.

"I'm doing just fine, sir," I replied, while doing my best to keep my answers short to conceal the pain of his tight grip.

Before long his grip became unbearable and I knew that he knew, that my excuse to use the bathroom was my way of tapping out without looking weak. When I made it to the restroom, better yet recovery room, I closely examined my hand for bruising. He gripped my hand so tight, that it felt like I had a bad case of arthritis. I could hear Moses' squeaky mop bucket making its way down the hallway towards the restroom.

"Is everything okay in there?" Moses asked. "If so hurry up because I have a restroom to clean!"

In my deepest voice, I replied, "Yes, sir!"

I walked out the restroom, and there was Moses with the mop handle in his hand.

"Follow me," he said. I walked slowly behind Moses along side his staggering shadow. "I would normally move this by myself."

Moses was the kind of man who might just offer to give his doctor a checkup.

"Do you need help moving these boxes?" I asked.

The boxes didn't look heavy, but I kept my opinion to myself. I got ahead of Moses's orders and started moving the boxes to the nearest closet.

This was a breeze, I thought feeling good about helping him.

Moses didn't say a word as he stood watching me like a supervisor. After moving and stacking up all the boxes, I dusted my hands off. Moses thanked me and then pointed to the twelve barrels of cleaning chemicals that needed to be moved to the waste pile. Each barrel weighed anywhere from 50 to 100 pounds.

"That's what I needed help with, Clifford," said Moses.

"A five-year-old could move those light boxes and stack them in a closet," said Moses. "Oh, but if the barrels to heavy for you Clifford, I can handle it myself. I've been doing the tough work around here for the past fifty years. One more rep won't hurt this old man."

"Of course I don't mind," I said as I cracked my knuckles.

I thought to myself, *There was no way old Moses could move those barrels by himself.*

"Is there a hand truck?" I asked.

Moses pointed down the hallway to the dolly. I took one step in the direction of the dolly and heard Moses calling me weak underneath his breath. I quickly turned around, carried those barrels along with my pride, what a heavy load. Moses stood nearby eating potatoes chips while watching me struggle.

I was exhausted. My body felt as if I had worked overtime but it was just the beginning of the workweek. I stood there sweating like a cold glass of water. After the last barrel I made it clear to Moses, that I wasn't doing any more lifting. Moses asked me to follow him to his office. After all these years I had never seen his office. I envisioned a small room, with a chair and desk and old broom handles hanging on the wall like plaques. Moses unhooked his large keychain from him belt buckle so he could open his door. He had a key to every room, including a key to my office. I was impressed that he could manage all fifty keys on one key chain. Not once did he look confused to which key opened his office door. To me, they all looked same.

When Moses opened his door, I was shocked to see that his office was much nicer than mine. This was no janitor's room. This looked like the office of a CEO. There were no brooms hanging from the walls, neither were there any traces of dust on the ceiling fan.

"Have a seat," he said, while walking behind his mahogany desk.

Even the guest seats where nice.

"Don't sit there," said Moses.

He invited me to sit behind his sacred desk.

"Thank you, Moses, but no thanks," I replied.

Something didn't feel right about sitting behind another's man desk.

"Have a seat," he said, like a stern father demanding that I sit in the seat he suggested.

"Yes, sir," I said while watching him pull the seat from under his desk for me.

"Sit back and relax," he said. I relaxed and reclined in the soft leather chair. The view was perfect. Moses's office looked like an exhibit, displaying the history of the company.

While chatting with Moses, we were interrupted by a phone call. Since I was sitting behind his desk, I answered.

"Hello, Moses's office," I said, but there was nothing but silence on the other end.

I was very familiar with the sound of my co-workers' voices. I could hear the person on the other end breathing.

"This is Moses's office," I said, but this time I deepened my voice to sound like Moses.

"Great Grandpa, is that you?"

I put the phone down and whispered to Moses that his grandson was on the line. The young man sounded as if he was on the cusp of puberty. By the look in Moses's eye, he was extremely excited that his great grandson had called him. While Moses was on the phone, I walked around his office admiring what I was seeing. But also, I was eavesdropping on his conversation with his grandboy.

I remember the feeling of my son calling me at work just to let me know how baseball practice was. Listening to them, felt all too familiar. I shook Moses hand and let him know that I was leaving so I could get to church.

"My grandboy hit a home run," Moses said with joy.

I smiled and whispered to Moses that I would catch up with him later. Hearing Moses's conversation with his grandboy, ironically or not, gave me hope and put a little joy in my heart. Leave it up to God to use a man named Moses to give me hope on the hope I'd tried to navigate things with my father.

Twenty minutes later I turned onto the street where my church was, I could hear the choir competing with the birds. Melodies sung in unison with clapping hands and foot stomping. I could see the congregants swaying together through the stained glass windows. The view from the parking lot looked like I was watching an organized musical.

To keep from being noticed by the deacons, I hid in the balcony on the last row. The pastor would have to possess the eyes of God if he were going to shine the light on me from so far away. I sat back observing the service like a guest, enjoying the choir as if this was my first time hearing them sing. Each note sung felt like a sincere expression from the bottom of their souls, ushering in sounds from the place where only angels dwell.

I spotted my wife smiling, singing and rejoicing with her hands raised giving adoration to God. Many times I prayed, asking God to give me a heart like hers. Just the thought of God's goodness would bring tears to her eyes. The last time I cried in front of my wife was at Junior's funeral. So, I guessed I'd better stay disconnected until God picked up his line.

I departed from service the same way I'd entered, unnoticed. I felt good, even though I only stayed for a short time. The truth was I was more excited to eat some good chicken and listen to music, rather than sit and listen to a sermon. There were similarities between a juke joint and church. But on this particular day I preferred grooving to a John Brown backbeat while a bluesy soul singer demanded I move my feet.

There was a thirty-minute drive to the diner. While driving I rehearsed my favorite tunes as if I was headed to a recital. I wanted to be prepared, just in case I was put on the spot to sing. The audience was so impressed the last time, that I felt obligated to perform some new material. Within a few miles from the diner I felt anxiety creep up my spine like a weed, and I started choking up, singing out of tune and coughing after every stanza.

The street was dark. No neon lights or signs stating the diner was open for business were lit. In fact, all of the businesses on the block seemed to be locked up. If it weren't for the light poles every few blocks, it would have been hard to see the sidewalk. I parked my car and walked up to the building to take a peek. I could see that the kitchen light was on. It was difficult seeing through the dark building so I knocked on the glass door, hoping someone would answer. I remembered I had a flashlight in the car. I still had my work clothes on so I assumed it wouldn't look awkward flashing a light into a dark building.

"Put your hands up!"

I'm busted, I thought. I dropped my flashlight and placed both hands on the glass door. Because I was nervous, my palms started sweating, which made it difficult to keep my head on the glass door.

"Spread them!" the voice commanded.

At that point I wasn't sure if I was being robbed or the police were really trying to arrest me.

I obeyed the command, while thinking to myself that I should have stayed at church. I prayed silently as the stranger frisked me. The stranger shined my own flashlight on me. I tried turning around to see who it was, but the light was blinding.

"Who are you? Are you from around these parts?" the voice asked.

I made sure that I responded with Southern politeness, and in a non-aggressive tone.

"No, sir. I live on the other side of town. I stopped by to see if the open mic was happening tonight. A good friend of mine invited me last week."

"What's your friend's name?" he asked.

I hoped that mentioning Nathaniel's name would help me out.

"That name sounds familiar," he replied. He asked me to describe Nathaniel.

"He's about 6'3 and about 270 pounds, black male. I'm assuming he's in his seventies, but he could be younger," I said.

The only reason I guessed Nathaniel to be in his seventies was because there was something vintage about his soul. The light dimmed and the stranger asked me to turn around. I was scared out of my mind, so scared that I froze.

"Are you going to kill me?" I asked.

"Just turn around, Clifford," he said. I turned around slowly as if I had severe lower back and neck problems. While looking at the ground, I noticed how huge his shadow was. The type of shadow that kept company with giants.

"Clifford, it me," said the stranger.

"If you stop acting like an old man and turn around you will see who it is," he said.

This must be my father, I thought. He was the only man I knew personally who talked with such a commanding tone. We stood face to face but I couldn't make out the details of his face. He had on a baseball cap that hid his eyes. After a few seconds he removed the ball cap.

"Nathaniel," I said, while shaking my head in relief.

I told Nathaniel he was lucky I didn't wet my pants, while shaking his hand and feeling grateful he was someone I knew. He went on to lecture me about what normally happens to strangers that shine flashlights inside dark buildings that obviously have a closed sign on the door.

"What closed sign?" I asked.

Nathaniel pointed at the closed sign that was right in front of me. If the closed sign were a right hook, I would be picking my teeth up off the ground. The sign was right at chin level, but I hadn't seen it. I was so anxious to enjoy the open mic session that

I forgot the jam sessions were held only on the first and the fourth Tuesday of the month.

"Are you hungry?" asked Nathaniel.

Other than the music, the fried chicken was the other incentive to come to the juke joint.

"Good music doesn't fill an empty stomach," I said.

"Ride with me," Nathaniel suggested.

I had no problem riding with him. But the last time we rode together I felt like a hostage in my own car.

I asked Nathaniel if he didn't mind walking, if the place wasn't too far away. He agreed to walk.

We ended up at a twenty-four-hour dinner that served some of the best sardines and grits — the best alternative to fried chicken — that I'd ever had. The walk there and back wasn't bad either, and I still got home at a decent hour.

When I arrived home, my wife had a surprise waiting for me. It was as if she knew, exactly what time I was coming home. The temperature was perfect to sooth away the aches accumulated after a hard day's work. While sitting in the tub, I thought about all the interesting things that happened that day.

"How was work?" she whispered, as she eased through the cracked bathroom door.

If I had a hard day at work my wife would sing and wash my back while I sat in the tub. She dimmed the light and lit a candle. I sank deep into the tub as If I was being baptized, hoping to come out a new and refreshed man. She sat next to me on the edge of the tub and dipped the washrag into the water and started gently washing my back as if she could feel the soreness herself. I asked her to not leave but to stay so we could spend some time alone. Ever since our son's death we hadn't talked much about it.

Remaining silent had become our way of copping. Even sleeping in the same bed didn't feel the same anymore, even though we kissed every night before bed. Cold hearts didn't keep us warm at night.

"I miss him," she said. "There's not a day that passes by that I don't replay the nineteen years of his life. Some nights, I dream of being pregnant with him all over again. The sensation of his feet and hands pressing against the inside walls of my stomach, how I tickled his unborn feet. Sometimes, I still feel the weight of him in my arms and whispering to him how beautiful he was. Those labor pains were nothing to pain of the emptiness I feel now," she said with tears running down her face.

I remained silent and listened to her pour out her heart. This was the first time since the accident that we'd cried together, no longer pretending to be strong for one another. With both arms she hugged me from behind and rested her head in the crevice of my back. I felt her tears running down my spine. Even though she held me tight, she felt more like a strong wall of support for me to lean on. Because we mourned in the arms of one another a piece of our soul was restored, and even though we were mourning together it reminded me of our first date. We unashamedly poured out our souls to one another.

Still, there was something I was holding back. At the time I didn't feel it was best to share with her that I was seeking counseling. I didn't want to appear weak in front of the one I was suppose to be strong around. I also didn't want her to feel anything less than a super woman. I assumed she would take it personal and feel inadequate by not being able to nurture my pain away. But I knew sooner or later I would have to open up and tell her.

I like to tell myself
You are the sun,
the set and the rise.
You make sure
My garden continues
To bloom, 'til we reunite

Man, I know you're going through
Tough times; I'll be your path
When the roadway ends; be your light when darkness wins; call
when you need a hand, I'll pick you up, be your best friend, your
kin; we're brothers in the end, brothers till the end

The next morning I woke up about an hour earlier than usual, contemplating whether I should go to work this week or take a few days off. I felt the urge to schedule another appointment with my counselor. There were so many things that happened the previous week, and I didn't know how to interpret what was going on in my life. I felt emotionally overwhelmed.

When my mother would get stressed, she would say quotes like "Sometimes you don't know whether you're coming or going, but one thing for certain, you have to keep moving." My mother's quotes were stitched into my soul. I was still barley functioning, putting one foot in front of the other to survive daily medial tasks. If I didn't open my soul to someone, I felt as if I was about to explode. I hoped my counselor was prepared.

"Good morning, this is the office of Dr. — "

I interrupted, "Nathaniel, is that you?"

We started chatting like old friends, reminding each other of how good the food was from the other night and our projection for upcoming baseball games. We chatted so long that I forgot the reason I called and hung up as if the number I called was Nathaniel's personal home number.

When I came to my senses and called back, I asked Nathaniel to schedule me another appointment to see my counselor. Nathaniel obliged and then asked if I would pick up a prescription for him from the pharmacy, which was near my house. Usually what the old folks called "meds" were a pack of cigs.

The next morning I woke up extra early so I could be the first person in line at the pharmacy. It dawned on me that I didn't remember Nathaniel's last name.

"Welcome to Johnson's drug store," said the clerk.

I asked the kind clerk to direct me to the pharmacy. He kindly walked me to the back of the store where the pharmacy was and I shook his hand and thanked him for being so helpful.

"No problem, Brother Clifford," he said.

Honestly, I hadn't pay much attention to the clerk's face, but after staring in his face for a second, I realized we were both members of the same church.

He mentioned that he enjoyed my singing and asked if I would lead the devotional services next.

"What are you doing here so early?" he asked.

I explained that I was picking up a prescription for Nathaniel. The mentioning of Nathaniel's name made the young clerk eyes light up as if there was a long history between the two. I assumed Nathaniel might have been more than a frequent customer. Judging by the clerk's smooth baby face, maybe Nathaniel was his uncle, coach, or mentor.

He went behind the counter and after a chat with the pharmacist, before long I had Nathaniel's prescription in my hand. The young clerk and I walked back to the front counter so I could pay. While reaching in my pocket to grab money, he tells me Nathaniel's prescription was free.

Stunned by what he said, I asked what type of prescription is free. I was curious to know what was in the bag.

"Oh! Nothing but some joint medicine and cream," he replied.

"That makes perfect sense," I said aloud.

Before asking his name I caught a glimpse at his nametag and noticed his name was Nathaniel too.

"Thank you, Nathaniel. I'll be sure to tell Nathaniel you said hello."

I arrived to my counselor's office just a few minutes early. While walking up the steps towards the office door, I notice a sign hanging on the doorknob: "Will return in 15 minutes."

I sat on the steps and watched the pedestrians walk by with their coffee in one hand and briefcase in the other, arms swinging and legs trotting to the rhythm of their attitude, some smiling, others frowning. Needless to say, it was an Otis Redding "watching tide roll away" kind of day.

"Good morning, Mr. Alexander, would you mind if I slide through and open the door."

"Good morning, sir," I replied while moving out of his way.

Judging by the countenance of his face, he looked to be having a great morning. I'd guessed Nathaniel would be welcoming me, not my counselor.

"Would you like a cup of coffee?" he asked.

"Sure, with two cream and sugars," I replied.

While he was in the other room preparing the coffee, I started snooping around his office, looking closely at portraits and accolades on his wall. There were several framed pictures of different families, some were propped on his desk, while others hung from his wall. Out of all the pictures, I couldn't find anything in common. No common ancestry, neither did any sets of eyes look the same. Usually in a man's office, there's at least one picture of his family. The counselor wasn't in a single picture, which I thought was strange.

I did notice one book that stood out amongst the others on his shelf, only because the spine of the book was in the opposite direction. There was a photo sticking out the book separating the pages like a bookmark. In the picture, there was my counselor sitting with a little boy on his lap. The little boy looked four years of age. My counselor and the little boy both had dusty brown hair with blue eyes. Because I could hear my counselor making his way back to the office, I hurried to put the book back on the shelf.

"Here's your coffee, Mr. Alexander."

"Thank you," I replied and took a sip.

"Where's Nathaniel?" I asked.

"He had to step out to go pick up a prescription. He said he was confident his good buddy would forget."

I laughed at this. But Nathaniel considering me as his good buddy made me feel good. I let the prescription remain inside my coat pocket. It would be a pleasant surprise for Nathaniel to know I stuck by word and picked up his meds.

"Are you comfortable?" asked my counselor. "You seem a little up tight."

"No sir, I'm comfortable and doing just fine," I replied as I slouched back into his sofa, patiently waiting for a series questions.

It wasn't long before the yellow memo pad crept from behind his desk. He placed the memo pad down on his desk and walked over to his file cabinet and pulled out a manila folder with my name on it. He calmly walked back over to his desk, while looking inside the folder. He sat down, and then removed his glasses and stared at me.

"Why are you really here?" he asked.

I was a little thrown off by his question.

"The last I checked, it's the sick who need a doctor," I replied sarcastically.

After sensing that I was offended, he started to explain himself.

"I can feel your internal strength, Mr. Alexander, and it's obvious that you deal with your pain privately."

"I didn't become this way over night," I replied. "Life circumstances groomed me this way. I embraced my position as the big brother, father, friend, church member, husband, supervisor, the list goes on. The callous on my soul grew thicker year after year and time never slowed for the sake of my pain, but no pain I've ever experienced can compare to losing my child."

My counselor sat there and listened to me patiently as I cried unashamedly, as if I was the only person in the room. While sobbing my heart out, I felt a strong hand on my shoulder. It felt as if a trusted friend was confronting me, and there he was, Nathaniel handing me some tissue. I didn't even notice he'd walked in. I guess I was sobbing so loudly that I didn't hear the doors hinges squeak. I quickly wiped my face. I reached in pocket and handed Nathaniel his prescription. Nathaniel thanked me and then left the room. A part of me wanted to follow Nathaniel out and forget about my counseling session. I wanted to play a pickup game of chess. But I couldn't because I was here for one reason only. So, the question continued and I was running out of tissue. The macho man inside taunted me like a bully. *Real men don't cry,* echoed in my brain

My counselor's questions were deep and penetrating, and my heart was under arrest while my behind was glued to the seat. I felt like Nathaniel was listening on the other side of the wall, peeking in every minute or so and watching me like a guardian angel as I bared my soul to a stranger, in whom I hoped had answers.

"Are you mad?" my counselor asked.

The once comfy chair now felt like I was sitting on needles.

I stood up and repeated aloud the question he'd asked me.

Whether he was prepared for my answer or not, I was not going to hold back any emotion.

"Am I angry? Am I angry? Of course I'm angry," I said as I pounded his desk with the same intensity as two boxers' gloves in a prizefight.

My words were just as intense. Not only did I want my counselor to hear me but also feel the pain in my soul.

"You're damn right, I'm angry!" I yelled.

I felt like a fool trying to bargain with death, as if death ever returned a soul.

"I want my son back!" I shouted to my counselor.

My request fell on ears that had no power to honor my petition. With my fist clinched tightly, I pounded his desk again.

"Give me my son back!"

He remained calm, as if he was comfortable in dealing with hostile patients. My blood pressure had risen which led to a throbbing around my temple. I finally calmed down and sat back in the comfy chair.

I looked my counselor directly in his eyes and shared with him the truth of my agony. I was mad at God and didn't know what to do about it.

I recited Psalms 139:8, the psalmist makes the observation about God omnipresence: "If I go up to heaven, you are there; if I make my bed in hell, you are there. Hello, my name is Clifford, is God in the other room?" I mumbled those words under my breath because my mind couldn't comprehend what was spewing out my soul. I felt like a blasphemer for letting the words "angry with God" come out my mouth.

"Imagine spanking your child and then expecting them to pray to you to heal the wounds that you created," I said to my counselor.

Just that thought alone prevented me from sleeping most nights, waking up feeling like I had just been in a fight. The day felt like a waste of time. I started out feeling optimistic, only to end up feeling hopeless.

Right before making it to the front door, the counselor stopped me and handed me a blank yellow memo pad. I turned and looked at him as if I was trying to block a dirty hand from touching a white suit.

"What is this for?" I asked.

He asked if I'd ever tried journaling. He thought it would be best if I wrote my thoughts out on paper, even the thoughts that I was ashamed to express verbally. He empathized with me and also expressed that I was in for a difficult task but that there was light at the end of the tunnel. I agreed that I would at least make a good attempt at journaling.

While walking down the office steps I decided to walk in the opposite direction from where my car was parked. For some odd reason I felt like walking towards the right even though I was headed in the opposite direction from where I was parked. I was nine blocks into my journey when I noticed a small coffee shop. Instead of going inside I sat down on the curb and looked at the blank page of my new journal and began to scribble down any random word that flowed through my mind.

My thoughts didn't flow in any sequence that made any sense so I soon gave up. My penmanship was just as distorted as my emotions. It would take God to interpret this missive. Trying to convince myself to leave and go home, a kind gentleman sat a fresh cup of coffee next to me and then asked if I was a writer. I hurried and put my journal into my coat pocket. In my mind I felt he might have been peeking over my shoulder trying to see what I was writing.

"No, sir, I'm no writer."

"You looked like you could use a friendly cup of coffee," he said with a grandfatherly smile on his face.

He was short in stature with a red beard and a strong accent that was obviously from another country.

"Forgive me for assuming coffee was a writer's best friend," he stated.

"Your name, sir?" I asked.

"Call me Russell," he replied and we shook hand and departed.

I went right and he went left. After a few steps I turned around and watched Russell as he walked away, waving and smiling at each pedestrian that passed him.

Halfway into my walk back to my car, I revisited the yellow memo pad, my new journal and jotted down a few more thoughts. Because my head was down I mistakenly bumped into a man carrying his precious young son on his shoulders.

My initial thoughts where to act out of character and blame the man for bumping into me, even though it was most likely my fault. But after seeing the young kid holding on to his father's neck with all his strength, I apologized and helped them pick up there belongings. With sincerity I apologized. He kindly accepted my apology as if it was a compliment.

While gathering the man's belongings, his young son jumped on my back and locked his arms around my neck. His father was surprised by his son's actions and started to chastise him, threatening him with a potential spanking. I assured the young father that it was okay. When my son was his age he did things like that all the time," I said.

"Have you ever ridden a horse?" I asked the young boy.

"Yes, sir," he replied with a big smile, showing off his chubby cheeks and freckled face.

I held my arms out and allowed him to climb my limbs all the way up to my shoulders. He held on tight, with his arms wrapped around my neck and his feet curled around my waist. I started bucking like a horse and he held on as if the pavement was brewing with hot lava. I could feel his little heart pounding through my back and ironically we were on the same beat. We were both excited.

The young lad asked kindly to sit on my shoulders. Because I stood about seven inches taller than his father I assumed it to be the reason the young'un was so excited. Now he could brag about being taller than his old man. Either way, I was okay with doing whatever it took to contribute to the youngin's excitement. The kid's father and I talked briefly. He was a young father and recently married man, doing his best to provide for his family while caring for his wife who was diagnosed with breast cancer a few months earlier. Nevertheless, he didn't show any sign of self-pity. I could see glorious faith illuminating from his soul, penetrating my heart. We had a lot in common, both being rooted in spiritual traditions. His light was certainly shinning bright.

Because our time was short, the young lad horsy ride had to come to an end. His father made an attempt to remove him but he started to cry and hold on tighter to me. The young father was embarrassed but I reassured him it was okay. In that very moment I felt God was up to something. I slowly got down on my knees and placed my hands on his so I could bargain with him. He relaxed and let go. He slowly walked around so we could look face-to-face. This moment felt all too familiar as I stared into his dark brown eyes. He gave me the biggest hug and said thank you. His arms were too short to wrap completely around my back but he tried his best.

"No thank you, son," I replied and reached into my coat pocket and handed him a piece of candy and two dollars.

Surprisingly he refused the candy and took the two bucks. He hugged me again and then ran to jump back onto his father's shoulders. He knew where home was.

The warm coffee couldn't compare to the warmth of that child's heart, earnestly trusting in his father's ability to be strong and carry him through life. I felt like God was hugging me with the same hands that upholds the universe but used this child's arms to lift my feeble soul.

While walking back to my car I pulled out my yellow memo pad and wrote: "I couldn't let God go even if I tried."

I noticed that Nathaniel was leaving the office. He fumbled with his keys, appearing to be in a rush to get somewhere. To get his attention I yelled his name from across the street but he didn't hear me, so I jogged across the street hoping to catch him. It appeared as if he was running from me, which I thought was strange. He kept running but then I noticed that his arm was waving as if he was trying to flag someone down as well. He slowed down after a few blocks or so, and I was finally able to catch up with him. I was out of breath, bending over with my hands on my knees gasping for air.

"Nathaniel," I said again with a faint voice.

He turned around and realized it was me and patted my back,

making sure I was okay.

"I don't need a pat on the back," I said. "Where's the water?"

He laughed. I asked if his prescription had been right.

"Of course. How else would I be able to move with such speed and agility," he said while staring down at me as if he had just beat me in a race.

After regaining my breath I told Nathaniel that I had about an hour to spare and asked if he wanted to catch up on a game of chess at the local park. Nathaniel suggested that we play in the waiting room back inside the office. I didn't want to play at the office, considering I had just left there. But Nathaniel insisted on playing at the office. The guy who Nathaniel was trying to catch earlier had left his wallet and Nathaniel wanted to stick around just in case the man realized his wallet was missing.

"We don't have to worry about Doc because he's on lunch break and his next patient isn't for two hours."

"Would you like something to drink?" Nathaniel asked while pulling out the chessboard.

"Of course I want water," I said sarcastically.

Nathaniel laughed and walked back into the break room. While Nathaniel was away I tiptoed my way back into my counselor office. I knew it was wrong, and I wasn't sure what I was looking for. I walked over to his bookshelf looking for the picture. I remembered it being hidden in one of his books. Pictures say a lot of things to those who listen, and I was all ears.

The picture was dividing two chapters like a bookmark. I

looked over my shoulder before grabbing the book hoping not to get caught being nosey. When I opened the book, I realized it was a Bible, which led me to assume that the particular section of the Bible gave meaning to the picture.

When I was a kid, I remember my mother placing things she cared about—her family and things she worried about—in the crease of her Bible. If she had something particularly worrisome, say an unpaid bill that had grown too high and caused her stress, she would place it in her Bible, next to the scripture that offered: "God shall apply all my needs according to his riches and glory." My mother would say something like, "If it's over my head, it's still under God's feet," and then close her Bible and smile and kiss me on the cheek.

The picture was rested in the second chapter of Joel. I wasn't a Bible scholar, neither could I recall the Sunday school teacher lecturing about Joel. Job, Jeremiah, John, and, of course, Jesus were the only "Js" that were significant to me. But I noticed Joel 2:25 was underlined with a yellow highlighter.

"What are you doing over there? The chess table is in the lobby," declared Nathaniel.

I lied and told Nathaniel I was reading one of the magazines I read earlier at my counseling session. He asked me to hurry because he was anxious to play. Nathaniel walked back into the lobby, which granted me a few seconds to put everything back in place. While placing the book back on the shelf I mistakenly dropped the picture on the floor. The picture slid underneath the desk, so far underneath the desk that I had to get down on my knees to grab it.

On the back of the picture read "RIP until we meet again." Shocked by what I read, my heart started to ache. Instead of placing the picture back between chapters two and three of Joel, I put the picture in my shirt pocket.

Doing my best to conceal my grief, as soon as I noticed Nathaniel sitting confidently at the table, I yelled out, "The champ is here! The champ is here, and down goes Frasier!"

I took my seat, cracked my knuckles and suggested he make the first move.

My palms were sweaty. Deep down I was feeling regret for being nosey. Nathaniel was normal, but I was too disturbed to focus on the game. It's hard to maintain a poker face when trying to play chess under pressure. I decided to ask about the picture.

Nathaniel seemed to have no idea about what picture I was talking about. His only concern was my next move. I asked again but he didn't pay me much attention. I tried to relax and just play the game but I couldn't focus, so I reached in my pocket to pull the picture out. But right before laying the picture flat on the table, we were interrupted by my counselor. We both were surprised to see him back so early.

I thought to myself how embarrassing and disrespectful it would be if he looked at the picture regularly and found out it was no longer in his Bible. I hurried and tucked the picture back into my pocket.

Because I was guilty I felt that my counselor could see through my shirt pocket and see the picture. It's kind of like leaving your driving license home and assuming that every police officer that drives by you intuitively knows you don't have your license. I waved at my counselor as he walked by. With every step he took closer to his office the more sweat ran down my forehead.

"Is everything okay?" Nathaniel asked while laughing.

I knew he thought he was getting the best of me at this chess match.

"Mr. Alexander, Nathaniel's a pretty good chess player," said my counselor before closing his office door.

Once I heard the door close, that was my sign to make a quiet exit. I asked Nathaniel for a rain check. He agreed, but not without letting me know how bad he'd been beating me. He asked if I could come back by later that night, after hours because he would be there doing some cleaning.

"Absolutely," I said.

That would be the perfect time to replace the picture. We agreed on a time, shook hands and then I left. No sooner had I walked out the door, then I quickly ran around to the side of the building hoping I'd be able to sneak a peek into the counselor's office. I was certain I looked like a criminal trying to claw my way up a brick wall. The window was too high for me to get a good look in, plus it was too much of a strain trying to hold myself up on a brick wall with only a few protruding bricks. Luckily there was a pile of cinder blocks across the streets. Though I would have preferred a ladder, I had to use what was available. Both him and Nathaniel were sitting across from each other inside the office, but oddly Nathaniel was sitting in the counselor's seat.

Nathaniel stood up and walked over to the bookshelf. If he picked up the Bible to look for the picture my plan was to come clean. Deep down in my heart I felt that Nathaniel knew exactly what picture I'd been talking about earlier while playing chess. The Bible stood out about two inches from the other books. He grabbed the book right next to the Bible and that's when I was finally able to breathe. I couldn't make out what book he was handing to my counselor but there appeared to be a trusted bond between the two. Nathaniel handed the counselor the book and he tucked it underneath his arm. They shook hands and then my counselor walked out. I quickly jumped off the cinder block and walked in the opposite direction. I hid around the backend of the building and peeked around to see in what direction my counselor headed.

After a few minutes I stood back on the cinder block to take a sneak peek hoping to see what Nathaniel was up to. There he was sitting behind the counselor's desk with his hands behind his head and his feet propped up on the desk. Because I heard music playing softly, I leaned in closer to the window hoping to hear what song inspired him to sit in such a relaxing position. I couldn't make out the lyrics, but it sounded like old hymns playing from a record player. Halfway through the song he reached in his pocket and grabbed his pocket square. I assumed his glasses needed cleaning. But after removing his glasses I saw tears running down his cheek.

Nathaniel was expecting me to come back to the office later to continue our game of chess. But after seeing him cry, I decided to call first. Fortunately for my sake there was a nearby pay phone, only about four blocks away. The phone rang, but no one answered. By the third call, Nathaniel answered. Well, at least I thought he did. It was strange that I heard his voice but the phone was still ringing.

"Hang up the phone," he said.

Like an idiot I continued talking while the phone was still ringing, thinking some stranger was behind me suggesting that I hurry up and finish my call. I slammed the phone down on the hook only because I felt like the guy behind me was distracting me.

"Stupid phone," I said aloud. I turned around, and there he was, Nathaniel, smiling and asking me what did the phone do to deserve such bad treatment.

"How did you know I was here?" I asked.

"I have the eyes of the Lord," he said, with his bifocal glasses on. "The chessboard is set up and ready," he said as we started walking back towards the office.

After entering the room, I noticed that the chessboard wasn't set up in the lobby anymore. Nathaniel stood at my counselor's office door and invited me in. At that moment I felt like I was being summoned to the principle's office. The guilt grew on me with each step. I was hesitant to take a seat, so I slowly walked around the office closely examining the pictures on the wall. I didn't want to jump right in and start playing chess. I wanted to get a feel for things.

Nathaniel sat there comfortably as if he was in his own living room. There was one particular framed picture that stood out to me. The picture was saying so much that I grabbed it off the wall and asked Nathaniel about the people who were in it. There were three women in which I thought to be really good friends but not related. One lady was African American with very dark unblemished skin and a radiant smile. She stood on the left. The women in the middle looked Native American. Her skin tone was olive and her hair was long and wavy, so long that her hair stopped at the small of her back. The wrinkles in the corner of her eyes made here appear to be the oldest. The women on the right looked the most interesting of the three. Her complexion was a caramel hue and she had big pretty eyes. It felt like she was looking directly at me. The color of her eyes was unreal, nothing like I've ever seen before. It was hard to take my eyes off of her brownish blonde eyes.

"That's my daughter," said Nathaniel, and the other two women are my wife and sister."

"Lucky man," I said and I continued complementing him on their beauty.

Nathaniel grabbed the picture frame from my hand and started explaining the significance of the picture. He couldn't resist smiling as he shared stories about what it was like being the mediator between his three ladies. He mentioned how impossible it was to win an argument with his wife. On rare occasions she awarded him the victory, he never considered her anything less that his personal angel.

"Beautiful like an angel but with a sword in her mouth," he said while raising his eyebrows and shaking his head.

I understood exactly what he meant. "My mother would spank you in the name of Jesus and then turn around and hold and pray for the pain to go away."

"What about your daughter?" Nathaniel ask.

"Where do I start?" I said, as I reclined back into the chair as if I was in yet another counseling session. "She can be mischievous, but she's smart. Got a good head on her shoulders, heading to college soon. She has big dreams. We've always been close. She's a daddy's girl, but then she's right close with her momma too."

Relaxed and reclined in the chair, watching the ceiling fan rotate, pleasant memories flooded my mind and I couldn't resist asking Nathaniel to put some music on. Because of the generation gap between us I reassured Nathaniel that I could relate to whatever music touched his soul. To my surprise, he put on some Al Green.

"You got good taste, Nathaniel," I said while nodding my head to the groove and singing along with the first verse.

"I'm a hard worker. Providing for my family has always been my priority. Joy filled my heart when I could provide vacations for my kids. Whenever I grew tired from the long hours at work and felt like giving up, images of my family enjoying a little luxury pop up in my mind." I tapped my foot on the floor to make sure Nathaniel was still listening.

"We have a lot in common," he said.

"My wife's a little more indulgent. Junior, especially, had a personalized key to his mother's heart. Junior was wise at using his key to my heart sparingly, but then he never did get in much trouble. Lord, I made it my job to keep Junior in line. Raising a Black child, especially a boy, sure ain't for the meek."

Nathaniel and I continued to chat until the doorbell interrupted us. I was anxious. My only goal was to return the picture.

"Expecting company?" I asked. Nathaniel remained calm and took his time while walking to the front door as slow as possible. The repeated doorbell rings and aggressive knocking didn't phase Nathaniel one bit.

"Should I answer the door?" I asked.

As soon as Nathaniel left the room to see who was at the door, I jumped up and walked to the bookshelf to put the picture back. All of a sudden I heard loud, boisterous laughing. It was so loud I got nervous I dropped the picture beneath the desk again. While bending down to find it, I saw two pairs of feet headed back into the office. Because I panicked I banged my head trying to escape from under the desk. Nathaniel yelled my name from the other room.

"Be right there, just tying my shoe," I replied.

I pulled my pants leg up and placed the picture in side my sock up around my calf area.

I couldn't make out the conversation but whoever it was sounded familiar. After the stranger peeked around the door, I knew my intuition served me well. It was Roy.

"I know you're in there," he said sounding like a police officer.

"Come out with your hands up!"

I followed his orders and stood up with my hands up.

"Busted," I said, and then we laughed and shook hands like old battle buddies.

"You guys want to head over to Jake's on Main?" Nathaniel asked.

Roy offered to drive.

"Front seat is yours," he said as he opened the passenger door like a gentlemen on a first date. I let the door remain open until both Nathaniel and Roy were both seated. He leaned over from the driver's side and asked whether I was going to walk or ride. I shut the door and then reopened it and sat down in his junky car.

"I better not get any milkshake drippings on my nice shoes," I said while trying to make room for my feet.

Roy revved his engine past the red line, as if he was trying to prove his little Ford Escort was a muscle car. I turned around to look at Nathaniel and we both burst out laughing at the same time.

"Those no horses under this engine, those are ponies," said Nathaniel.

Nathaniel and Roy went back and forth trading jokes. Within a few blocks of Jake's you could hear notes shooting off the stage into the atmosphere.

"Who is that?" I ask. "Man, he had that guitar screaming. As the old blues cats would say, it was talking to me."

This cat played the blues violently, as if the cat that ran off with his girlfriend had been closer to him than a brother. Blistering-fast guitar licks flowed like a fully loaded automatic rifle. His notes hit you right in the heart. I asked Roy to hurry up and park. I wanted to catch this guy before he ran out.

"No rush, Clifford, he never runs out," Nathaniel assured me. "He's going to be there for a while."

Before walking into the bar, I stood staring through the big glass window. The view from the back of the stage was just as good. I felt the glass vibrating to the pulse of the backbeat groove the band was playing. I didn't recognize the tune but it felt as familiar as a Sunday school hymn.

"Preach, Mr. Guitar Man, preach!" I said as I joined Nathaniel and Roy.

They gave a few amens, like congregants at an African American Baptist Church. Because Nathaniel was a favored regular we sat close to the stage. So close I could see sweat pouring down the band members faces as they made their way through a rendition of "Playing Hard for the Money."

The place was packed and full of energy. I was surprised the majority of the staff remembered me, even the cooks waved from the back of the kitchen. I felt like the hometown hero. I noticed a few familiar faces in audience. Some secretly pointed at me while whispering in their neighbor's ear. I hoped those whispers were compliments not complaints.

My server remembered my first and last name, and the song I sang. Even though I didn't remember her name, I did remember her motherly smile.

"Would you like the usual?" she asked.

"Sure," I replied, folding my menu and handing it back to her.

She leaned over and whispered, " I want to hear you sing one tonight."

"Yes, ma'am," I replied.

Even if I didn't feel like singing I knew I had to. What kind of man would I be if I denied her request, considering she remembered my name and the meal I ate the last time she saw me.

Nathaniel patted me on the back and chuckled.

"Did I miss something?" asked Roy.

Nathaniel took the honors in briefing Roy on what happed the last time we were there. Nathaniel also took liberty of embellishing what really happen. According to him, I was on my knees begging like a brokenhearted soul singer, tugging at the hearts of the lonely women in the audience.

"Clifford, you can't sing! You can barley whistle," said Roy. "Don't you know I hear you at work trying to hold a note?"

In my defense, Nathaniel went on bragging about how good of a singer I was. I did my best to ignore Roy and focus on the young cat playing the blues.

I leaned over and asked Nathaniel about the young cat on stage. It was evident there was something very special about the kid. He played guitar as if there was an untold story beneath his fingertips.

"I'll introduce you to him after the first set," said Nathaniel. Nathaniel hinted at the two of us doing a song together but I declined.

When my food arrived I was prepared to chow down. The steam

was escaping from my plate as if the chicken hopped right out the pan onto the plate. For a split second I forgot who was joining me at the table. The last time I ate around Roy, we ended up wrestling like boys on the playground. Roy pretended to take a grab at my plate. I grabbed my fork and asked politely whether or not he valued the hands that God had given him.

I couldn't wait to meet the young guitarist. There he was leaning on the wall with one leg propped, holding his guitar.

"Is that a Gibson 335?" I asked the virtuoso.

"Yes, sir," he replied while pointing at the headstock of the guitar.

He handed me his guitar assuming I would noodle around on it.

"Amateurs don't play around with a genius's tools," I said respectfully and handed him back his guitar. "Looks vintage! Is that a fifties' model?"

"Pretty close," he replied, "but actually it's a '65."

I was curious to how this young cat got his hands on such a precious axe.

"What's the story behind that beauty?" I asked.

"Actually it was my father's, sir. He gave it to me before he died. Knowing that my father's hands were on my guitar the last night he was alive reminds me to play with conviction. It sort of feels like we're playing together."

He turned the guitar around to show me the wear on the neck of the guitar. It was obvious this instrument had many miles on it.

His guitar case was covered with stickers as if the case was previously owned by either a soldier or a Peace Corps worker. I thought maybe the kid's father was a hippie.

"Would you like to hear the story behind this guitar?" he asked.

Seeing the excitement in his face made me even more eager to listen. I asked if he would mind if we stepped outside from the noise because I didn't want to miss any details.

He started by explaining some of the stickers on the case.

I was correct. This guitar had been all over the world, passing through many checkpoints. On the back of the case was a beautiful picture of a young couple who appeared to be in love. By the way they looked at each other, this was romance headed down the aisle of matrimony.

"That's me right there," he said.

I was confused until he pointed at the stomach of the woman who just happened to be his mother. I looked up at the kid and stared in his face and noticed an obvious resemblance.

"Yep! that's my old man," he said. "He was drafted to fight in Viet Nam. Not long after being deployed my mother picked up a second job, so she could afford to purchase my dad his dream guitar. What a lucky man, dream girl and dream guitar. My mother told me that during lonely nights my dad would hold the guitar as if it was her."

He opened the old guitar case and handed me a folded letter. You could smell the age of it. The letter was fragile with worn creases. I'm sure the letter had been read hundreds of times.

"Are you sure you want me to the read this?" I asked. He responded with a nod.

Dear Sweet one,

I've been missing you like crazy and things over here aren't getting any better. Nights get cold and lonely. But the guitar has become my trusted friend since being away from you. I've learned how to play the blues and some say I can make the guitar "talk" a little.

I can't wait to see you and my baby boy's face. Oh how I wish I were there to play melodies to the both of you.

If you get a chance go purchase the album by the Beatles called Abby Road. Listen to the song "Oh Darling." It's a pretty hip tune that makes me think of you. A few weeks back the Beatles visited our fort and sang a few tunes. They were pretty hip for white guys with funny accents.

I hope my boy turns out to be a musician, so make sure you two listen to a lot of good music while he's still in your womb.

Love you and miss you,

Your Man

"My mother discovered the letter years after my father's death.

I was about four years old or so, and I was snooping around my mother's closet and found this guitar case. I dragged it from the closet and opened it. I didn't think it looked like much other than something to bang on. There were loose strings and a few guitar picks in-between the strings. It didn't keep me from plucking away. When my mother saw what I had done, she spanked me. My heart hurt because I was separated from my new toy so I ran to the other room and cried my little eyes out. Later my mother sat on the floor next to my bed with the guitar resting in her lap and asked me if I wanted to play. With tears still on my cheek, I plucked on the strings. She asked me to sit next to her and that's when she rested the guitar in my lap. Even though the guitar was twice my size it felt comfortable. While plucking away, my mom found the folded letter tucked behind the velvet lining of the guitar case.

"You can still see the watermark from where her tears smeared the ink. Because I was so young, I didn't understand exactly what was going on, but I knew what I was feeling. It felt like my father where sitting right next to me. A moment with a man I've never met nor will ever see: my daddy.

"I carry this letter in my guitar case wherever I go. I've read this letter so many times that I can recite it from memory. But it's still something magical about holding the letter in my hands and reading it. My mother says my voice sounds just like my fathers. A part of me feels I speak on my father's behalf every time I perform."

Jonathan's story moved me. There was conviction and sincerity behind every word he spoke. He spoke as if the unfortunate events surrounding his early childhood propelled him to live and play his music with a sense of purpose, never taking a note for granted. I noticed Jonathan gazing across the room as if he could see his father clapping and cheering him on.

"Is everything okay?" I asked.

"Everything is just fine," he said putting his arm around my shoulder.

He directed my attention by pointing in the direction of what I thought was a mirage.

"What am I looking for?" I asked.

All I saw was a crowded room of smiling faces and full stomachs. He leaned in closer to me and directed my attention toward the kitchen. I didn't have the best set of eyes and squinting didn't help either.

"Look closer," he said. "Look at the lady waving in the back by the kitchen door."

"Isn't she one of the servers?" I asked.

"Yes, sir," said Jonathan, "but she's also my mother."

I couldn't believe just seconds ago I was holding the precious love letter between the beloved and deceased. Immediately I recalled how sweet Jonathan's mother was the last time I ate there. Her hospitality was sincere. She made the diner feel like my mother's living room. She made sure my stomach was full and my glass of sweet tea never ran low.

Jonathan waved for her to come over.

"Hey, Mr. Alexander," she said while reaching for hug.

The warmth of her hug made me feel as if I was Jonathan's big brother. I could feel enormous strength in her gentle hands. The type of strength that can move life's mountains with a single comforting word. She looked into my eyes and sensed the pain I was concealing with a smile.

"Mom!" Jonathan said. "I let Mr. Alexander read the letter."

Neither was ashamed or embarrassed to know their past was shared with a complete stranger. At that moment I felt like family. Jonathan's mom didn't say much but I knew intuitively that both of them had found peace with their past. She went back to the kitchen but first requested her son play her favorite tune. Jonathan asked me to join him and I couldn't refuse.

Jonathan and I sang and played tunes all night. We played so long that the only people who remained at closing were the staff and, of course, Nathaniel and Roy. I sung myself hungry while Jonathan earned new callouses. After clocking out the staff sat down and yelled out request. Because we were having so much fun we took the challenge. Jonathan and I knew lots of songs; they were stored in our souls. After about thirty minutes of taking request someone yells from the back of the room to play a gospel song called "Precious Lord."

I looked through the remaining audience to see who would request a gospel song at this late hour. The gentleman stood up and walked closer to the stage. To my surprise it was my counselor! He was the last person on earth I expected to see. Just when I thought my vocal chords where loose, my throat felt like it was filled with egg yolks. The last time I heard that song was at my son's funeral, and there was no way I could pull it off with out choking up. I noticed Nathaniel leaning over and whispering something in my counselor's ear.

"How about some Sam Cooke?" my counselor yelled out.

The remaining staff chanted, "Sam Cooke, Sam Cooke ..." and I agreed to sing.

It looked as if Nathaniel had, yet again, saved the day.

We sang until midnight. After the second Sam Cooke song, my counselor left. He waved good-bye in a certain manner as if this wouldn't be the last time we see each other. For a brief moment on stage I felt like the doctor or, better yet, the preacher ministering to my counselor. It felt good to deposit a little love into his soul. Singing Sam Cooke songs had a way of making you feel like being in love. I didn't know the type of relationship my counselor had with his wife, but she'd be a lucky woman if those melodies stayed stuck in his head until he made it home.

Jonathan's mother packed two extra plates on the house. She knew it would be in my favor if I didn't arrive home empty-handed. I couldn't thank her enough.

She declared aloud, "You worked hard for the food."

Roy ended up catching a ride home with one of the servers. I think he had the hots for her; his eyes were on her all night. It would be Nathaniel and me on the road alone once again. Before leaving, I asked Jonathan if he needed any help carrying his equipment out to his car. I understood the burden of carrying heavy guitar amps and drums after a long gig. The guitar amp was usually the heaviest piece of equipment that required you to have a strong arm and good balance. Luckily his car was only a couple feet from the front door. Jonathan seemed to be a grounded young man and even though his father was deceased it was evident he had a good support system.

Nathaniel asked me to drive but I declined at first. I didn't want to be held responsible if anything happened to his car while I was behind the wheel. Nathaniel implied he was tired; he repeatedly scratched his eyes and yawned. I grabbed the keys and got behind the wheel.

"What did you think about tonight?" I asked.

Nathaniel popped in a cassette tape and asked me to be quiet. It didn't take long before I realized what I was listening to. Jonathan has his own record!

"I knew I should have got that kid's autograph," I said.

The drum groove was funky and his guitar riffs danced around the bass line. My fingers tapped along the steering wheel as if I was a ghost member of the band.

"No record deal yet, but, we hope to get his demo in the right hands," said Nathaniel.

Jonathan's music needed to be shared with the world. After listening to the first two songs on the tape, Nathaniel asked me to pay very close attention to track number 3. Track 3 was a love ballad with the dreamy sounds of the Fender Rhodes playing softly underneath the lead vocals.

"This song makes sense," I said aloud.

"The song is all about the love letter between Jonathan's mother and father."

Listening to the song made me feel as if I was next to Jonathan's dad while he wrote the letter.

"What all do you know about Jonathan?" I asked Nathaniel.

He chuckled for a few. I didn't think anything was funny about my question. But I was accustomed to his unpredictable behavior and sense of humor.

"I consider Jonathan my son," said Nathaniel.

Nathaniel sat erect and cleared his throat. "I'm responsible for raising Jonathan."

Shocked by what I heard, I got off the nearest exit, which was only about a mile away. I wanted to take the slow route back so no detail would go unspoken.

"Are you his stepfather?" I asked.

Questions upon questions flooded my brain trying to figure out the link between Nathaniel and Jonathan. Nathaniel just continued to laugh at the fact I was confused. We reached a traffic light and I told Nathaniel if he didn't start explaining himself, that I would put the car in park when the light turned green.

"The story isn't complicated," said Nathaniel. "The young guitar player's father was my battle buddy. Not only did we share the same battlefield but also the same barracks, bathrooms, and an occasional brew."

While listening to Nathaniel's story, my mind replayed the first time I met him on the doorstep of the counselor's office. I remembered him having a fearless aura about him, the kind of man that made negotiations with death with a smile on his face. He had a euphoric handshake that made you feel as if those hands had been touched by the divine.

"I knew the kid's father just as well as his mother did," said Nathaniel. "We lay back-to-back many nights in the trenches. It's easy to get acquainted under those circumstances. We met at basic training and later were stationed together. We didn't become close until the night he saved my life.

"One night we decided to sneak off fort after curfew. It was my idea. There was a bar a few miles away filled with women who loved military men, and I was in need to be in the presence of something a lot softer than machinery and explosives. Jonathan's father agreed to join as long as he established the terms. He wanted to bring his guitar. He was always practicing in his spare time, but he hadn't yet played in front of anyone. I never thought he had aspirations for performing. I thought playing guitar was a hobby. I agreed to cheer him on even if everyone in the crowed booed him. My main concern was meeting single ladies and doing what soldiers do.

"We knew we were close to the bar when we could feel the music we'd heard from a distance. Jonathan's father had confidence in his stride once we walked in to the bar. As for me, my eyes roamed the bar looking for that one young lady who was looking for a guy like me to flirt with. I noticed from across the room, this super fine lady. She had curves in all the right places along with a smile that commanded your legs to walk in her direction. In other words, she was hard to resist.

"While making my way over to her I was caught off guard by the master of ceremony. 'Welcome to the stage, Mr. John Wallace.' Not many people clapped. But once I turned around and realized it was my buddy I whistled and applauded loud and proud. I took the privileges of sitting in the vacant seat next to the young lady. I introduced myself as John's good friend.

"John had a voice like Smoky Robinson. He blessed the stage for an hour, singing the top 40 hits of our time. On the choruses the crowd joined in unison, especially the ladies, singing the soprano parts as if they were getting paid. John handled himself like a veteran performer, captivating the ladies but without making the fellas jealous. As soon as John finished singing all the ladies made their way to the stage except the one who I had my eyes on.

"While John was busy mingling with his new admirers, I sat next to my new lady. She smelled just as good as she looked, which inspired me to get closer and put my arm around the back of her chair and get close. She appeared to be having a great time. She laughed at my jokes and didn't find it offensive while I gently rubbed the small of her back. Thanks to John for setting the mood, lovemaking was in the air.

"After about an hour of sipping on scotch we were both ready to feel each other's lips. I was struggling just to keep my hands to myself. I whispered in her ear and asked if she minded if we stepped outside. As we got up from the bar I looked through the crowd for John. There he was sitting at a table full of ladies.

"And then, a booming voice shouted, 'Where's my woman?' My initial thought was that one of those women surrounding John was this drunken man's wife. 'Where's my women?' he screamed, but this time he got everyone's attention when he revealed he had a baseball bat and started making threats.

"My new date grabbed my hand, and hissed, 'He's crazy. I didn't think he'd find me.' About then he spotted us and started charging in our direction. He kicked through the tables that stood between us. He took a swing at me and out of nowhere John hits him with his guitar. We didn't bother to see if the guy was knocked out cold. We ran out of that juke joint as if it was about to explode.

"The guitar you saw his son playing was the same guitar that saved my life. If you take a closer look at the body, you'll see cracks in the paint. They don't call guitars axes for no reason. John chopped wood that day. We ran non-stop for about a mile, and as soon as we reached safety, I bear hugged him unashamedly, wrapping my arms around him as if he was the savior of the world.

"That night I learned three valuable life lessons: presumption, assumption, and consumption. Never presume a woman is single. Never assume a woman is yours for the night. And never consume too much alcohol. It makes it very difficult to run fast.

"That night, I lay back on my bunk and considered the worst that could of happened if John hadn't stepped in. Two days later, John died. Every day I wish I could of returned the favor and saved his life. His integrity was solid, and his heart was heroic. During my time as a soldier all I thought about was fighting war and making love. John somehow knew he was going to have a son. Every day he talked about the type of husband and father he wanted to be. I asked him how he knew. He said, 'God told me.' He said his son would call me Uncle Nate. Unfortunately John never got the opportunity to see and hold his son.

"On the delivery date I made sure I was there. After the baby was born the nurse addressed me as Uncle Nate and welcomed me into the delivery room. She handed me the baby. He had his father's eyes. With John's son in my arms, I looked towards heaven hoping that God and John would hear me. I prayed, 'God give me wisdom to lead this child and the strength to provide and protect.' I promised John I would take care of his kid as if he was mine. I was holding a gift from God. I felt this was my way of saving John's life and from that day I've enjoyed every moment of it. For the first few years I didn't get much sleep, not because of a crying baby but rather my mind trying to make sense of everything.

"One day little Jonathan asked, "Why did my dad die before I could meet him?' Jonathan was only about seven or eight years old at the time, but his soul was much older. He fully understood that a part of him was missing. His question hit me hard. There was no way to prepare for a question like that. I took a deep breath and silently prayed to God for wisdom. With deepest sincerity I answered, 'I don't know. But I do know that since you've been in my life, you have taught me what living really means.' He turned and looked out the passenger window. 'You're good to me, very good to me,' he said.

"To hear those words from a young'un will forever be stitched into the fabric of my soul. That moment was for me a glimpse into eternity, the place where time fades away and joy is perpetual. My mother's favorite Bible verse was, 'Knowing that all things works for the good of those who love him.' I loved this kid and this kid loved me. I knew he trusted me and rested in my ability to be the male influence in his life. It's been a privilege."

That was one of most heart-felt stories I'd ever heard. The car ride home felt like church. You know, the part during the service when someone's so overwhelmed by God's goodness that they have to stand and testify. Nathaniel had just shared his testimony with me, and it felt like God was sitting in the backseat enjoying the ride.

When I arrived home I was shocked to see my wife and daughter sitting on the front steps. I turned my high beams on so I could see exactly what they were doing. My daughter appeared to be resting on my wife's lap. Something looked wrong. The closer I got to them I could hear my daughter weeping. My wife waved for me to come closer. I sat at my daughter's feet while her mother rubbed her head.

"What's the matter, baby?" I asked.

I knew it had to be bad if she was crying in her mother's arms. If she didn't want to talk with me being around, I was perfectly fine. It's only certain things a woman can relate to, and my daughter was in good arms. I got up and kissed her on the forehead and told her that I would be inside if she wanted to talk later.

Before I could make it through the front door she called out, "Daddy, I'm going to be a single mother."

"What do you mean single mother?" I asked.

Connie whimpered, "Daddy, I'm pregnant."

That night Connie fell asleep between my wife and me. I didn't sleep at all. I knew Connie had met someone named Richard earlier that spring, but I barely knew the kid, had met him only once, and through the funeral and subsequent weeks, I hadn't seen or thought much about him. My thoughts were bumper to bumper like five o'clock traffic. *How could I have missed this?* I thought. All I could see before me was yet another set of problems and challenges, as they arose with the morning sun.

I had planned to meet Junior's girlfriend for breakfast. It was hard enough living day to day and accepting the reality that one of my two children was gone, much less worry about how anyone else was dealing with my and my family's loss. Even though I cared for his girlfriend Brooke, I didn't feel as if I had much to offer her. We hadn't spoken since the funeral, and, truthfully, a part of me was content with not speaking. She'd lost a boyfriend, but I'd lost a son. She's pretty, intelligent, and would find a new boyfriend in no time, but a father, a father will never find a new son, not ever.

BACK TO THE CHORUS

I planted lilies for you,
Paid them to the angels
When the day comes my life is through,
I can be with you

Why are things I have
The things I hate?
Gotta get rid of these demons
Help me release the weight

Brooke was an aspiring artist, which helped explain why Junior grew so attached to her. I married a singer so I certainly understood the connection, and she certainly had his attention. He and I hadn't often talked about girls or dating until he met Brooke. He asked for advice when it came to things concerning their relationship. She made him feel like being a better man and I was proud of that.

Brooke and I agreed to meet for breakfast at a nearby diner. She was late. I assumed, like most nineteen-year-olds do, she lived by a different clock, so I went on ahead and ordered my food. A man named Will recognized me. He'd been part of the EMS team that transported my son to the hospital the day of his accident.

I asked him to sit with me while I waited on Brooke. He pulled up a chair. I flitted around the usual small talk before I dove into asking the question I'd been waiting and wanting to ask. I'd gotten the call that my son was thrown off his motorcycle while I was at work. I assumed that maybe he'd suffered some minor bruises. I had no idea then of the extent or the severity of his injuries. I desperately wanted to know if he'd been conscious when EMS first arrived.

"Well, I — " Will started, then stopped hesitantly.

"It's okay. I can handle it," I said.

"When we arrived the woman who'd hit him was holding him. She kept saying over and over that she was sorry. In the ambulance he went in and out of consciousness. He was able to mumble a few words. He repeated the word 'hope' maybe five times. By the time we made it to hospital, he was unconscious. With the swelling on his brain, there wasn't much we could do besides keep him stable and give him oxygen."

Hope? Sadly I had no clue to the relevance of the name. When Brooke arrived, Will made his exit. For some reason, that Junior was conscious brought me comfort, and yet, I couldn't shake the idea that his murmuring "hope" was some sort of clue, but to what,

I would never know.

Brooke wasn't her bubbly self. To break the ice, I asked her about her parents. I didn't know much about her parents except that they trusted their daughter with my son. She kept her words short, while avoiding eye contact with me. I tried to be considerate. I remained patient hoping God would give me the right words to help her relax.

While she looked at the menu I asked her about the first time she met my son. She looked up at me and blushed and then looked down at the menu.

"Well..." She took a deep breath, looked up at the ceiling with young romance in her eyes, and then blushed. To see her reminisce with joy eased my sorrow.

"On most Saturdays I visit my aunty, who lives on the street behind yours. She's up in age, so I help her with housecleaning. One afternoon, my aunt asked me to pick up a few things from the corner store near your house. While walking back, I heard music blasting. It sounded like a block party. George Clinton and the Parliament were blaring. I had to see what was going on. There he was washing his motorcycle. I didn't want him to see me, but it's kind of hard to run backwards when you want to look forward. I noticed the name on the mailbox, so when I got home I asked my aunt. She's fond of y'all. When Junior was younger, he used to cut her grass. I couldn't wait until the following Saturday. As usual, I went to my aunt's house. As soon as I got there she stopped me in my tracks.

"'You don't look like you're here to work,' she said. She was suspicious. I tried to act normal but when she complemented me on my perfume, I gave in and told her everything. I can't lie, I was nervous. I thought she was going into the other room to call my mother but she came back with nail polish and a comb. 'Let me help you, baby,' she'd said. While she painted my nails, she told me about her first date with my uncle and how I should conduct myself in the presence of a man. She never asked me whom I was getting dolled up for, but I think she knew.'"

Brooke blushed again. I coaxed her to tell me more.

"I walked to the convenience store and tried convincing myself I wouldn't be disappointed if I didn't see him outside washing his motorcycle. I glanced down the street to see if he was there, then I stalled, looking at magazines and slowly walked the aisles. After about ten minutes, I decided to head back to my aunt's house. Soon as I walked out the door, there he was pumping gas. I ran back into the store and watched him. That loud muffler on his bike was a clue he'd gone home. And, sure enough, when I walked past, there he was, sponge in hand. He was dancing, too, dancing as if no one was watching.

"I had no clue what I was going to say. If all else failed, I figured I'd would walk past the house and take the long way back to my aunt's. Maybe I would wave if he looked my way. He walked into the house, which made it easier for me to walk up the driveway. I hurried and ran to the front door, hoping someone else would answer.

"Your daughter opened the door. I know her from school. I mentioned my aunt was her neighbor, and that I'd seen the mailbox, and I thought I would stop by. We chatted, caught up on life and school. She asked about my plans for college, and then invited me in so she could grab some handouts about a school she was considering.

"She must have known, because Junior returned with the brochure. 'Here you go,' he said. I just stared at him, while he stood there. 'Do you want it or not?' he asked. 'Depends if you're going there,' I said. I didn't mean to say this out loud, obviously. My intention was to keep that thought inside my brain. My mouth chose otherwise. I was so embarrassed. He said, 'I'll think about it, Brooke.' I couldn't believe he knew my name!

"Well, Connie caught me staring at her brother while he walked away, so she shoved me out the door, demanding that I go and help her brother wash his car. While walking down the steps, I turned hoping I could retreat, but there she was on the other side of the windowpane giving me the thumbs up and laughing.

"At first Junior ignored me. I almost gave up. I was almost out the driveway before he said my name. I turned around and there was a wet rag headed for my face. He's lucky I have quick reflexes and caught the rag before it hit me. 'Don't just stand there, help me,' he said. And so I did. Well, until my aunt screamed from her backyard for me. He asked me if I wanted a ride home, and I said sure. He gave me a helmet and I hopped on the back and held on tight.

"Because my mother is strict, I gave him my aunt's phone number. The next week he asked me on a date to the state fair. Ever since then I've sort of felt like we were meant to be together. He had a way of making me feel as if I was the only girl that mattered."

"Did he ever mention anything about his and my relationship? I was always hard on him."

Her silence scared me. I could tell by her body language that my question made her uncomfortable.

"Never mind," I said. We could talk about it another time.

"Mr. Alexander, do you mind if I order another meal?" she asked.

"Order whatever you like," I assured her.

I waited patiently for her to finish eating while replaying in my mind what it had meant to be the father of a Black son. I had been hard on him — even with seemingly insignificant activities like walking over to a friend's house. I knew he's be judged first by what he was before he was judged by who he was. I taught him to be exceptional, and that meant taking his innocence away early and incorporating reality.

"Mr. Alexander, Junior admired you. He called you his hero. There were times he mentioned your expectations of him and how he couldn't believe that you were proud of him even when he made mistakes."

"Was there anything he disliked?" I asked. I was curious to know. There were things I'd done that I wish I had the power to erase from his memory.

"Well, sir," she said as she hesitated to open up.

"It's okay, I can handle it," I said for the second time that day. I continued, "There were times I was hard on him. When Junior got older into his teen years I felt there were things he wanted to talk about, but I was coward who had a lot of guilt. I know how close you and Junior were and I figured — "

"I know, sir, that he loved you deeply," she said.

"Would you mind sharing one of your best moments with him?" I asked Brooke.

"Do you remember the first time we met?" she asked, as tears ran down her cheek.

"Yes, I do," I replied. "Why was that particular day so important?"

"Junior had assured me that I was special because I would be the first girl to meet his parents. It makes a girl feel special knowing this. At the time I was working at a dry cleaners. He'd stop by and wait for me to get off. On the day I was to meet you and Mrs. Alexander, he walked in and blew kisses at me while I rang up a customer. He had an old military duffle bag in his hand, so I assumed he wanted some clothes cleaned. When I reached in the bag and flung the clothes into the laundry basket, he stormed the basket as if I'd thrown a 100-dollar bill in the trash. I fussed at him since he wasn't supposed to be behind the counter," she said and then stopped for a moment as if she needed to catch her breath after a long run.

"He always said we were two peas in a fussing pot." Brooke faltered again. "Anyway, he reached in the basket and unraveled the garment. He'd bought me a dress. He watched the counter while I quickly ran to try on my new dress. When I asked him how I looked, he said, 'Cute.' I said, 'Cute? That's it?' pretending to be sassy. He told me that dinner was at his mother's house at 7:00 and that he thought his mom and dad would think I was cute too."

"He was right." I smiled. "Both Mrs. Alexander and I thought you were right cute and right perfect for Junior. What I asked next took courage. "Did he ever mention anything about me purchasing his motorcycle?"

"Junior loved his motorcycle. He told me you'd surprised him when you pulled up riding it. He said it felt like Christmas in spring."

I hated that with all the details I'd covered with my son, all the nudging for him to walk the straight line and work hard — all the lessons about integrity — and that I'd tried so hard to protect him, to make him a man, and that, ultimately, it was the motorcycle I gave him that killed him.

Brooke and I chatted for another ten minutes. Then I walked her to her car. I thanked her for taking the time to open up to me. I had found solace listening to my son's sweetheart. I also realized there was no prejudice in sorrow and that there was comfort to listen without judgment to what comes out of another's heart. I opened her car door for her when it became clear she didn't feel well.

Just as I was about to ask her if she was okay, she bent over and threw up. I ran back inside the restaurant to get some water. By the time I made it outside she was already in the car and turning the key. When I made it to her, she'd slung open the driver's door and threw up again.

"Please let me help you. Should I call your mom?" I asked.

She started to cry. I pulled her to me as if she was my own daughter. She cried on my shoulder.

"Everything will be okay," I repeated over and over in her ear. She put my hand on her stomach and continued crying.

Touching her stomach took my breath away for a second. All of a sudden it hit me, and knowing that she was pregnant with Junior's child felt like I had been hit with an uppercut. I felt like I was standing in the corridor of life and death.

Clueless of how to respond and hoping to comfort her I started singing old gospel hymns. I offered her a ride home but she insisted on being alone. She said she needed time to figure out how she was going to explain being pregnant to her mother. I didn't know much about her parents, and only hoped they would be gracious to her.

I reached in my wallet and handed her all the money I had. She slapped my hand away.

"I'm not getting an abortion!" she cried.

I hated she'd assumed the money was for an abortion. I lay on the hood of the car so I could prove to her my intentions. Finally, she rolled down her window.

I explained to her that I wanted to be the first to contribute to diapers and his first baseball glove. She slowly got out the car.

"I'm sorry," she said. She seemed embarrassed.

"Apology accepted," I said.

So much was running through my mind. Later that day after I got off work I called my counselor. His office was only thirty minutes away. I thought if I dropped in he might make time for me.

When I arrived, not only was he there but Nathaniel was there as well. The light in my counselor's office was on. The closer I got to his window, it sounded like a counseling session was going on. The same brick I used to eavesdrop was still there leaning against the wall. It wasn't hard to recognize Nathanael's voice. His voice certainly didn't lack any bass. Instead of continuing to pry on their conversation, I quickly made my way around the building to the front door. The front door was cracked, so I didn't have to knock. I tiptoed in. No one was in the lobby. My counselor's door was slightly cracked, almost completely closed. There was an empty seat by the door. I decided to sit there until they finished chatting.

It sounded to me that Nathaniel's voice dominated the conversation. He was giving advice as if he were the counselor.

"How's Clifford?"

The mention of my name made the hair stand up on my neck. The door was cracked just enough for me to see inside. Nathaniel sat behind my counselor's desk looking rather dapper. He wore a wool sport coat with an oxford shirt underneath. His glasses barely hung on to his nose as he squinted to read the yellow memo pad. He mumbled a few words. He appeared to be checking away items off his list. It was hard to make out his facial gestures so I assumed he was checking off clients' names.

I tried to sneak out but failed. Nathaniel called my name before I could make it to the front door. I turned and pretended I was excited to see him.

"Nathaniel," I said loudly as I walked back in his direction.

We shook hands. I complemented him on how dapper he was, hoping to distract him from asking me why I was at the office.

"Don't want to hold you up from your hot date," I said jokingly.

Nathaniel asked why was I there. I quickly made up something about running errands for my wife. My counselor walked towards us. I kindly asked Nathaniel to excuse us for a second. I expressed to my counselor that it was an urgent matter, and that I needed to schedule an appointment as soon as possible. He was understanding and agreed to see me first thing the next morning.

While walking out of his office I felt relief. There was Nathaniel sitting on the doorsteps.

"Mind if I have a seat?" I asked.

"Sit down for what? I'm ready to go meet my hot date and I need a sideman," he said jokingly.

My initial plan was to go to Bible study but I preferred hanging with Nathaniel. I asked him to join me first at church. I wasn't sure if Nathaniel was a religious man, but it was clear to see that he possessed a light, the sort of light that's only given by the divine. I suggested that we sit in the parking lot and listen to the sermon from there.

"I thought the church was a hospital for wounded hearts." Nathaniel asked. "What are you hiding from, the law?"

I agreed by nodding, but I kept my quiet.

The parking lot was full. We arrived right on time; the choir had just started singing. Since everyone was on the inside, I chose to remain outside and sit on the hood of my car and listen. Nathaniel joined me, humming the melody while the choir sang. The sun had just set and there was just enough light left to see the stained glass windows of the church. Nathaniel got off the hood and started walking towards the building and asked that I follow. Even though I said no, I followed him towards the building. The worst thing that could happen, I guessed, was that I'd get noticed.

We were ten feet from the window when Nathaniel started clapping to the beat of the tambourine. He asked me to join but I refused because I thought he was being silly. He continued to clap and sing as if he was member of the choir. Maybe he hadn't been to church in a while, I thought. I sat down on the ground with my back against the brick wall fiddling around with loose grass waiting for him to finish. If he was feeling the spirit, I didn't want, as the old church mothers would say, to hinder it.

"Is that Pastor Williams?" Nathaniel asked. It was darn near impossible to see through the stained glassed windows.

"I can recognize that voice anywhere," Nathaniel said.

I wasn't paying much attention to what the pastor was saying but according to my watch, it was time for a selection from a soloist. I mentioned to Nathaniel that on most Bible study nights I sang throughout the services but lately I hadn't been inspired to sing.

"You don't have to be inspired to sing, all you have to do is open your mouth," said Nathaniel.

At first I thought it was a smart aleck reply but I couldn't argue with him because it made perfect sense. My patience was running short and my stomach growled, reminding me that I hadn't eaten. My initial play hadn't been to stay for the entire service but rather check in to ease some of my tension. I started walking back to the car hoping Nathaniel would hear my footsteps and get the point. I never turned to look to see if Nathaniel was following until I made it back to the car. He was still standing in the same place. I got in car and flickered the bright lights.

It didn't take long before Nathaniel headed back to the car. He actually started jogging to where I was.

"Get out the car, man. You have got to hear this," he said.

I tried to tell Nathaniel that I had been a member of church for majority of my life and there was nothing different or special about to happen tonight. He ignored me and dragged me out the driver's seat.

"Listen, man, don't you hear that?" Nathaniel said.

I had no clue what to listen for.

"Aren't you a singer? Can you not recognize a good singer by the way he pray?" Nathaniel asked.

I thought Nathaniel's statement was crazy and absolutely didn't make any sense.

"Listen closely," he said, as he pulled me closer to the window.

"Is that Roy?" I asked.

He nodded.

I blurted out of my mouth, "What in the hell is he doing at my church and why in the hell does he have a mic in his hand?"

I had to see with my own eyes what was about to happen. I was all but dragging Nathaniel. Once we were in the church we crept unnoticed to the balcony.

I sat in amazement. Boy, did Roy have vocal chops. His vocal riffs were soaked in the blues but this was no sad singing. He started the tune a cappella and before long the band picked up the melody and took the song to the next level. It was hard for me to hide. The song got good. I didn't feel no ways tired, and I stood up and started singing. Joyfulness jumped in my lap, and I felt like dancing. When Roy finished singing, Pastor Williams grabbed the microphone.

"What is this?" he said.

This made me laugh. Whatever it is that wouldn't let me hold my peace, well, I knew that the Great Physician was at work on my heart. I closed my eyes and allowed the good Lord to do what I needed him to do.

Pastor Williams asked the congregation to join him in prayer. "The scripture says that when one of us hurts we all hurt, and one of our dear brothers and his family is hurting during this season in their lives. So if you would grab your neighbor's hand and begin to petition our heavenly Father, ask that he touch the hearts of the Alexander family."

The mention of my name coming from his mouth created a

lump in my throat. I didn't know if he had spotted me in the balcony or God told him I was in the room. Either way I felt exposed and wanted to escape. Nathaniel's grip was firm, so firm that it would be hard to escape without making it obvious, and he didn't have plans of letting go until the prayer was done. I noticed a few members looking for me in the crowd. I kept my head down just in case Pastor Williams spotted me and thought my presence meant I needed or wanted an alter call.

Pastor Williams didn't pray long, but I felt that God was using him specifically for me that night. As soon as the congregation said amen, I whispered to Nathaniel that it was time to go. It wasn't so much that I didn't want to be at church but that I knew I would have to answer questions. This churchgoing flock had the best intentions and well-meaning hearts, but I didn't feel like opening up or even pretending to open up.

On the way out one of the young ushers noticed me. "Is that you Mr. Alexander?" he asked.

I was tempted to pretend I hadn't hear the usher call my name, but I replied, "Yes, sir."

The young usher gave me a hug. I was so caught off guard by his hug that I froze. I didn't know whether to hug him back or let my arms continue to hang by my side.

"I needed that hug more that you could imagine, Thomas. You're growing into a fine young man," I said with sincerity.

He reached in his pocket and handed me a folded letter. I promised him I would read it as soon as I got home. Thomas was a good kid. A few years younger than my Junior. Truth be told, Thomas didn't have the easiest lot in life either. His grandparents were raising him, and his grandfather had died the year before. I didn't know about the boy's mother or father, but, even so, for a grandson to bury his grandfather was the natural, rightful course to things. All the same, things were different for Thomas now, and different isn't always easy.

While I was walking back to the car, it dawned on me that I had left the headlights on in my car. I asked Nathaniel would he mind going to get Roy, hoping he had some jumper cables. While Nathaniel went looking for Roy, I sat on the trunk and borrowed light from the moon. I opened Thomas's letter. It read:

Dear Mr. Alexander,

I would like to thank you for all you have done for my grandmother and me. Thank you for your faithfulness and kind heart. Even though my grandfather was very ill and could barley communicate, trust me when I say this: your choir songs meant a great deal to him and eased his suffering. You made my grandfather's last days on earth better. The last Sunday he was able to attend services he told me he thought your voice was his preview of heaven. The day before my grandfather transitioned, he asked me to grab our baseball gloves and roll his wheelchair outside. He wanted to play catch. He struggled to throw the ball, but he did it

*with a smile. He mentioned remembering watching
you play baseball at the community parks. He bragged
about how strong your pitching arm was. He said
that I should ask you to teach me your curve ball.
Junior league tryouts are next month. I know there's
a lot going on in your life right now, but if you would
please teach me how to throw a curve ball I would be
grateful.*

Sincerely,

Thomas

"What are you doing, God?" I asked somberly. I stared into the moon hoping that God would sketch the answer in the sky.

Moonshine would be good right now, I thought to myself. But just as soon as I did Roy pulled his car beside mine and scared the hell out of me. The Italian Stallion was at the wheel and Nathaniel was riding shotgun.

"Heard you need a jump!" Roy shouted, then revved his engine.

To which I responded, "Brother Roy, that's one way to put it."

TAKE IT TO THE BRIDGE

And when it rains and it pours
tears from my eyes,
those sunrays they always peak through
I call you my silver lining.

I got the world staring me in the face
Everybody wants an answer
Nobody wants to wait. I hear what
You're saying; I believe your words true
These shoes I'm standing in
are walking miles I never knew

Even though my stomach growled, instead of going to grab a bite
to eat with Nathaniel, I asked for a rain check. The ride back was
rather silent. Because Nathaniel offered to drive I reclined in the
passenger seat and closed me eyes. Soon we came to a stop.

After not moving for what I thought was too long, I opened my eyes. Nathaniel had turned the car off. I didn't notice at first where we were, but then I realized that Nathaniel had driven us to the bridge where my son had his accident. He'd parked off the shoulder, maybe 500 yards from the bridge. Nathaniel and I got out of the car and walked half the distance of the bridge. Other than faint sounds from beneath the bridge and the subtle sounds of a draft against the leaves, the road was quiet,

"Why did you stop at the bridge?" I asked Nathaniel.

"Do you remember the family picture on the wall back at the office?" Nathaniel asked.

Nathaniel had a weighty look on his face as he waited for me to remember the picture, but for the life of me I couldn't recall any such photo.

"I never told you, but there was a person missing."

"Who?" I asked.

"Me. You and I have something in common," he offered. "I lost my son too. We were close, just like you and Junior. The reason I wasn't in the picture is because I wanted my family to get used to me not being around. Fathers who lose sons die long before we hit the grave. The day I met you I saw a strong man desperately trying to regain his strength. Roy had told me about you years before your son passed. Roy really respects you. Roy came into my life when I needed a son. It took a long time for me to see, but that's when the healing began. You will never forget the pain, and you will never stop missing your son, but the day you realize that, like me, God gifted you with a fathering heart is the day the pain will make sense. There are fatherless children who need a man in their lives with a fathering heart. Every time God allows me to be a part of young man's life, what's broken in me mends just a little."

"I can't, Nathaniel, I — "

"Clifford, do you know what was special about the juke joint diner other than the fried chicken? That juke joint isn't just a place for music and good food. It's a community of people who turned setbacks into soul music. God blessed me with a sense of purpose in life. A few years after my son died I went to school and got my degree in counseling. Clifford, I am sorry if I betrayed our trust. Like me, you were too tough to take advice from someone just because they have the initials DR in front of their name. The way you shook my hand on the first day we met, I knew you weren't looking for a counselor, but a friend." Nathaniel put his arm around my shoulder. "You are not alone."

I was speechless, and all I could do was cry. For the first time I felt like a burden had been lifted, a burden that had been too heavy to lift alone, and now I could breathe without bitterness strangling the joy from my heart. What a relief knowing that someone I knew could identify with a pain I couldn't describe. I didn't have much to say.

"You're never too old or too manly to hug," Nathaniel said and for the first time in a long time I was able to hug someone.

While walking back to the car I asked, "Nathaniel, I've a question for you."

"What's that?"

"Are you hungry?"

On the way to the diner I mentioned that I wanted to invite my wife, even though it was late. We made a quick stop, I called her, and she agreed to meet us. We arrived a few minutes before her and I sat patiently on the front row waiting for her to be by my side.

Even though, my wife meeting me for dinner was impromptu, the night was begging to feel like a planned date. She sat close to me, tucked under my arm as we listened to Jonathan serenade the audience.

"I love you. You are my strength," I whispered in her ear, as Nathaniel walked to the stage.

"We have special guests in the house tonight, so put your hands together for my good friend, Clifford."

I leaned in close to my wife and kissed her on the cheek.

"Surprise," I said.

While walking on stage I thanked Nathaniel. Jonathan put his guitar around my neck. The audience was silent. I tapped the microphone to make sure it was on.

"I'd like to dedicate this song to my wife. The past few months have been really tough on my family and if it wasn't for my wife …" I choked up a bit and then sighed. "I love you, baby."

FIRST VERSE:

When I see you crying baby, often I don't know what to say

Just know that when you're hurting baby, I can feel your pain

There's a reason why we are together, we were built for tough times

As long as I have you baby I want you by my side

CHORUS:

Let's hold hand and dance

Let's hold hands and cry

Let's dance the pain away through the night

SECOND VERSE:

Anytime we are together, you make me feel strong.

If I ever felt alone, I know I could count of you to lean on

I don't know what the end will be, but at this moment it's just you and me

Can I have your hand, may I have this dance tonight

CHORUS:

Let's hold hand and dance

Let's hold hand and cry

Let's dance the pain away

Through the night.

I asked Jonathan to continue playing the song as I made my way off the stage to dance with my wife for the first time in years.

ELISION

After death there are two songs.

I never liked the smell of hospitals. Even though the hospitals are sanitary, the scent of death lingers in the air like old garbage. The anxiety of a waiting room overwhelms me. Doctors are the bearer of bad news. So are priests.

Shortly after waiting in the lobby, the nurse got my attention. She asked if I was Nathaniel's son. I lied and said I was, so I could find out the details on Nathaniel's condition. She informed me that Nathaniel was admitted to the ICU. Hearing the words ICU made my blood pressure rise.

"What do you mean ICU?" I said, demanding answers.

"Nathaniel has had a heart attack," the nurse replied.

"I was just with him the night before and he was his usual self."

The nurse asked me to calm down.

"Mr. Alexander, Nathaniel is alive, but he not only had a heart attack but also — "

Just hearing the word "alive" felt nostalgic. I heard those exact words while looking at my son only moments before he took his last breath. I demanded that I see Nathaniel, who the nurse said would be moved to a private room very soon and that I could wait for him there.

When the nurse opened the door to the small dour hospital room, the first thing I noticed are Nathaniel's clothes balled up inside a plastic bag. The thought crossed my mind that maybe he was actually looking forward to going to heaven. As soon as the door closed behind the nurse, I told the empty room that I needed Nathaniel to survive for my sake.

When the door cracked open, I hurried and took a seat and then stood back up once I realized the nurse was preparing for Nathaniel to enter the room. I was scared to ask if was he okay, so I remained quiet. And then I heard Nathaniel's voice, though shaky, from down the hallway. I stood at the corner of the door so I could greet him with a smile. He appeared to enjoy being chauffeured.

"Move out of the way, Clifford, before this young lady gets distracted by your good looks and bumps these old legs of mine against the door," said my good buddy.

I helped the nurse roll him in.

"Want to see who can run the fastest now?" I said jokingly.

"Even with a bad heart, this old man will still beat you," he replied and we chuckled together.

While asking Nathaniel questions about how he was feeling,

he'd interrupt me and start asking about my family and making sure my wife knew where I was. At the time I couldn't understand why was he so concerned about me. I guess this is what separates average men from heroes; heroes put others first and lead lives of service.

"Why don't you have seat, Clifford?" asked Nathaniel. "I'm not going to die just yet, so relax."

I sat down in the chair next to his bed.

With a knock on the door, Jonathan arrives. I opted to leave the room but Jonathan suggested I stay. Nathaniel was excited to see Jonathan.

"Where's your guitar?" Nathaniel asked.

"Of course I have it," Jonathan replied.

I kindly asked Nathaniel would he mind if Jonathan and I stepped out of the room for a second to chat. After walking out the room I updated Jonathan on the seriousness of Nathaniel's health condition. With tears in our eyes, we hugged each other like brothers, knowing our time with Nathaniel might be short. Jonathan walked back to his truck to grab his guitar. We returned to Nathaniel's bedside, prepared to sing a few tunes but his eyes were shut. I remembered the yellow paper with my and Jonathan's name written on it.

"What's this?" I asked Jonathan.

He unfolded the yellow paper, read whatever was written on it, and casually placed it inside his coat pocket.

It was difficult for me to look at Nathaniel, as he lay there with tubes hooked up to him. There was so much I wanted to say to him, but I was speechless.

Jonathan grabbed his guitar, strummed a few chords and started to sing.

> VERSE 1: I woke up one Sunday morning, looked out my window
>
> I saw another brother struggling, he needed a helping hand to hold.
>
> Sometimes life feels heavy, sometimes you just need a friend, To help you carry on.
>
> CHORUS: I'm your brother, I'm your friend. I'm someone you can depend on. I can't see you struggling and call you my friend. When you call me brother just know you can depend on me.
>
> VERSE 2: Too much in life, To be handle alone If you ever feel burden just know I'm here to share the load.
>
> CHORUS: I'm your brother, I'm your friend. I'm someone you can depend on. I can't see you struggling and call you my friend. When you call me brother just know you can depend on me.
>
> THE BRIDGE: Put your hands in my hand, lets lift each other higher. [Repeat four times.]

While Jonathan was singing, I hoped Nathaniel could hear or at least feel the love in the room.

"What a great song you wrote for Nathaniel," I said.

"No, sir," said Jonathan, "I wrote this song for you."

"Why me?" I asked Jonathan.

"I'm not sure. I felt like I had to write this song," said Jonathan.

He reached inside his coat pocket and handed me the yellow paper.

Daily I visited Nathaniel at the hospital. We didn't have much conversation, he was always tired but that didn't keep him from offering me his smile.

On October 28, 1983 at 5pm I received a call at work to come to the hospital. As I drove, it felt like Nathaniel was riding shotgun,

"Everything is going to be okay," I could hear him say.

When I walked into the hospital, my wife ran to me. She was smiling.

"Is everything okay?" I asked.

"You're about to be a grandfather," she said.

The baby had come a month early.

When I got to my daughter's room, I felt like I was twenty-two again. My daughter called me over, held my hand tight and began to push. Seven minutes later I was holding my grandboy in my arms.

My grandson and I cried together as I held him in my arms as he took his first breaths.

"This boy got lungs," I said.

OUTRO

In death there is the love song we sing solo.

That winter Nathaniel died. During those final months we had, Nathaniel and I spent a lot of time together. We ate a lot of chicken and played a lot of music. Nathaniel possessed a peace within himself that was beyond my understanding. He wasn't worried about death. He wasn't concerned about anything other than living with a sense of purpose. The week before he died he joined me at church. It was my first time back singing since Junior died. Nathaniel had seen me cry plenty of times but by the time I finished singing, there he was standing, applauding tears of joy while thanking God. It was then that Nathaniel asked me to promise him that Jonathan and I would sing at his funeral. I kept my promise. Jonathan sang the first verse, and I sang the second.

DA CAPO

In death there is the other love song we sing together, its riff a perpetual canon — the round echo that leads its singers back to the bridge.

Jay probably grew tired of me telling him of the day he was born.

"Ironically your mother and aunt went into labor at the same time and at the same hospital Nathaniel was in. After you were born, I carried you over to Nathaniel's room and asked him for his blessing. I lifted you towards heaven while Nathaniel prayed for us. His last words to me: 'That child you're holding needs you.'"

Jay looked at me with his wonderment, his batter's glove on, ready for the game.

"I think often about Nathaniel's life and legacy. I think about how he served as a bridge in my life, a bridge

from the pain and despair to joy and purpose. Jay, you were born at the right time and having you in my life has healed me in more ways than you will ever know. Do me a favor at your game today. Keep your eyes on the ball. Base hits win games."

"No problem, love you, Grandpa."

All my senses were involved with a heightened sensitivity to the environment. There were bright lights and the scent of popcorn. Proud screaming parents stood at the fence cheering on their child with hopes buried in their heart of their child hitting the game-winning homerun. I watched closely as the next batter-up took warm-up swings. He kept his eyes on the pitcher and swung as he threw.

"Batter up!" the empire screams.

The score was 3 to 5, bases loaded with two outs at the last inning. Jay turned to me for approval.

"Keep your eyes on the ball, son."

"Is that your son?" asked the lady beside me.

"No ma'am," I replied. "That's my grandboy!"